FIELDS
OF
VISION

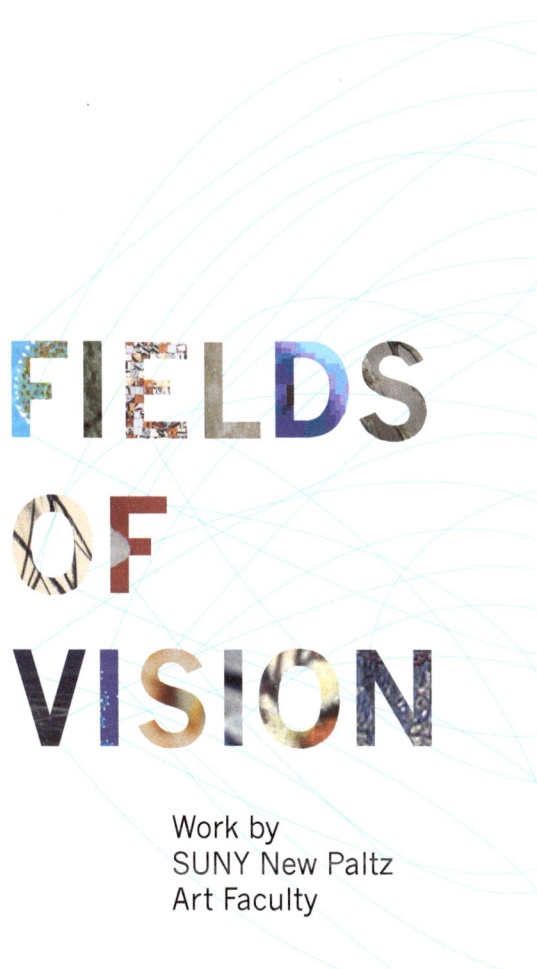

FIELDS OF VISION

**Work by
SUNY New Paltz
Art Faculty**

Thomas Albrecht
Robin Arnold
Jamie Bennett
Steven P. Bradford
Rimer Cardillo
Amy Cheng
Bryan Czibesz
François Deschamps
James Fossett
Andrea Frank
Matthew Friday
Kathy Goodell
Rena Leinberger
Carmen Lizardo
Ann Lovett
Aleánna Luethi-Garrecht
Myra Mimlitsch-Gray
Itty S. Neuhaus
Amy Papaelias
Jill Parisi
Jessica Poser
Emily Puthoff
Thomas Sarrantonio
Anat Shiftan
Suzanne Stokes
Alice Wexler
Cheryl Wheat
Jennifer Woodin

The Samuel Dorsky Museum of Art
April 13–June 23, 2013

This catalogue is being published on the occasion of the exhibition *Fields of Vision: Work by SUNY New Paltz Art Faculty* curated by Carl Van Brunt and on display at the Samuel Dorsky Museum of Art from April 13 to June 23, 2013.

Support for The Dorsky's exhibitions and programs is provided by The State University of New York at New Paltz and the Friends of The Dorsky Museum. Support for the publication of the exhibition catalogue has been provided by The State University of New York at New Paltz, School of Fine and Performing Arts.

Edited by Jaimee P. Uhlenbrock

Published by the Samuel Dorsky Museum of Art
State University of New York at New Paltz
1 Hawk Drive, New Paltz, New York, 12561

Designed by Anne Galperin

Printed by Lightning Source
Distributed by the State University of New York Press (sunypress.edu)
ISBN 978-0-615-70148-6

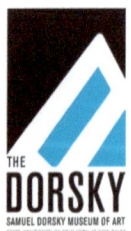
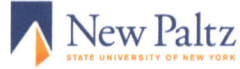

CONTENTS

INTRODUCTIONS

The Samuel Dorsky
Museum of Art
is pleased to present
Fields of Vision: Work
by SUNY New Paltz
Art Faculty, an exhibition
and accompanying
catalogue that feature work
by 28 Art Department
faculty members.

These faculty members teach courses in printmaking, photography, painting and drawing, sculpture, graphic design, ceramics, metals, and art education, as well as basic foundation courses. They are also professional artists and designers—and it is in that capacity that The Dorsky welcomes them to the museum with this special exhibition.

An exhibition of artwork featuring artists who live and work in a particular region presents a unique opportunity to look for similarities related to subject matter, style, and materials. Are there influences or themes that run through the work? Is there a particular style that seems to be characteristic of the Hudson Valley region or the SUNY New Paltz campus in 2013? This exhibition offers insights into the answers to these questions and more.

The exhibition also encourages campus faculty, staff, and students to see their colleagues and professors as artists and designers, not just teachers. Because it coincides with the presentation of work by art majors receiving their BFA and MFA degrees at SUNY New Paltz in spring 2013, *Fields of Vision* allows viewers to consider the relationship between the work of faculty and their students. We think that both the campus and the surrounding community will be impressed with what they see!

I am extremely grateful to Carl Van Brunt for accepting the challenge of curating this unique group show. I am also grateful to Dean Mary Hafeli for her leadership of the arts at SUNY New Paltz and her support of this exhibition, and to Anne Galperin, Chair of the Art Department, for her assistance in developing this exhibition and designing the catalogue. Thanks also go to The Dorsky's excellent staff—Daniel Belasco, Janis Benincasa, Wayne Lempka, Amy Pickering, Damian Scott, and Bob Wagner—for their support of this and every exhibition presented by the museum. Last but not least, thank you to the participating artists—our campus colleagues—for exemplifying in their own work the high quality of art for which SUNY New Paltz and The Dorsky Museum are known.

Sara J. Pasti
The Neil C. Trager Director

3

There is an old
Buddhist saying that
there are 84,000 doors
to the Truth.

We live in a moment when it seems that there are at least 84,000 ways to make art. This can be confusing and frustrating for artists and their audiences, or it can be liberating and a cause for celebration. Not too long ago, serious art was dominated by one or another doctrine, and the artist was judged to be either with it or hopelessly out of it. Thankfully, most of us are past that now. As an artist, gallery owner, and curator, I have come to embrace the multiplicity of ways artists do their work. I have learned to value open-mindedness above anything else. So it was with great pleasure that I accepted the invitation from Sara Pasti to curate *Fields of Vision: Work by SUNY New Paltz Art Faculty*.

In approaching my task I resolved to enable each artist to have enough work in the exhibition to give museum visitors a snapshot of the current methods and interests of the artists. I realized that with 28 artists in the exhibition this would be a challenge for everyone involved, including the hardworking and talented Dorsky staff. But having worked with them previously, I was confident we could pull this off. I also decided to make studio visits with every artist in the exhibition, so we could discuss in depth which works should be selected. These visits turned out to be incredibly inspiring to me. I came away from them greatly impressed with the intelligence, talent, and seriousness of commitment of every artist. As you will see, they reflect the level of accomplishment and variety of art-making that you might see in a visit to the galleries in the big city south of New Paltz.

In the spirit of this catalogue, which emphasizes visual communication over excess verbiage, this essay is brief. I urge the reader to spend some time perusing the works on view here, which make their case much more eloquently than I can. That said, I would like to share one brief story told to me by one artist in the exhibition. There were many such stories.

Not too long ago, the artist was in Iceland looking out towards the sea. An iceberg was floating there. The artist waited with her video camera and contemplated the iceberg, knowing that most of the big icy body was hidden beneath the sky-reflecting surface of the ocean. She was waiting for the iceberg to flip.

Making a work of art well may take years, or it may take no time all; it may mean doing tons of stuff, or very, very little; it may take mastery of craft, or it may eschew craft altogether; the work might be tragic, comic, ironic, or straight. It comes down to this: when the artist steps back, the work completed, beyond rationale, strategy, medium, or style, did the artist convey something worth contemplating. Did the iceberg flip?

Carl Van Brunt
Curator

It gives me great
pleasure to celebrate
the opening of *Fields of
Vision*, an exhibition
by 28 faculty members
in the Department of
Art at SUNY New Paltz.

The department, one of the largest at the College, has a long tradition
of excellence in creative production and teaching. Recent external
indicators—major faculty and student awards and noteworthy fellowships
over the past several years, a rise in national rankings—confirm the
continuing distinctiveness and quality of work done by our faculty and
students.

When I was an art student in the early 1980s there was always a great
deal of buzz and anticipation around the annual faculty exhibition. For
my friends and me, it was our one chance each year to see the recent
work of our professors—accomplished artists and designers well known
outside of the university, whose teaching and mentorship so immediately
impacted our own creative practice. Beyond its pedagogical importance
for students, *Fields of Vision* now on view at The Dorsky functions in

other ways as well. It provides a visual overview of the art department's curriculum-in-action, as individual faculty members' research and creative production, in large part, is linked to the teaching and learning that happens in art and design studios, classrooms, and labs. This faculty exhibition also serves other audiences throughout the College and wider community as an introduction to contemporary art ideas and practices. As the mission of the College is not only to teach, but also to create "new knowledge," it is entirely fitting that new knowledge in the form of art-based research and creative production done by the faculty should be shared publicly and prominently, and disseminated widely and frequently.

While diverse artistic sensibilities and approaches are essential to a dynamic and responsive curriculum for students, it is quite a challenge to select and juxtapose faculty works in such a way as to provide the viewer opportunities to forge meaningful connections among ideas, themes, material approaches, and functions. In *Fields of Vision*, The Dorsky, like some of its counterparts at other colleges and universities, wisely has opted to rethink traditional approaches in applying an inquisitive and responsive curatorial touch. Carl Van Brunt, curator of the exhibition, manages to honor the cacophony inherent in faculty creative production, while suggesting points around which some of these works and practices might be seen to cohere. In posing some areas of seemingly shared pursuits and divergent ends, and vice versa, we are invited to look for ourselves for convergences and divergences.

All of its other "presentation" functions aside, for the art faculty, the faculty exhibition is an all-too-rare and incredibly valuable exchange of, and conversation around, generative ideas of contemporary art and design—a "brown bag lunch" for sharing instances of essential, individual, creative production that transcend the day-to-day doings of committed art and design teaching and program service. I am honored to commend my colleagues on the work exhibited here and, as part of the campus community, I am happy to celebrate their collective accomplishments.

Mary Hafeli
Dean, School of Fine & Performing Arts

One of the most
rewarding aspects of
chairing the Art
Department is the
opportunity to become
well-acquainted with
the faculty's art and
design practices.

Collectively, these artists and designers work with a dazzling range of media, techniques, and subject matter. Pigments are made from PCB-contaminated Hudson River sediment. A paper flower quivers on a wall. Others grow 'round a vessel. A wall bursts into color. Type dances. Metal puddles and freezes. The rest of the iceberg stands revealed. A ready-made moves into another incarnation. The photographer imagines the work of another photographer. Sound emanates from sculpture.

These works and more by 28 full-time faculty in the Art Department at SUNY New Paltz are provocative, revelatory, and transformative. I'm delighted to experience them with you.

Anne Galperin
Chair, Art Department

WORK

Thomas Albrecht
Tinker, 2013

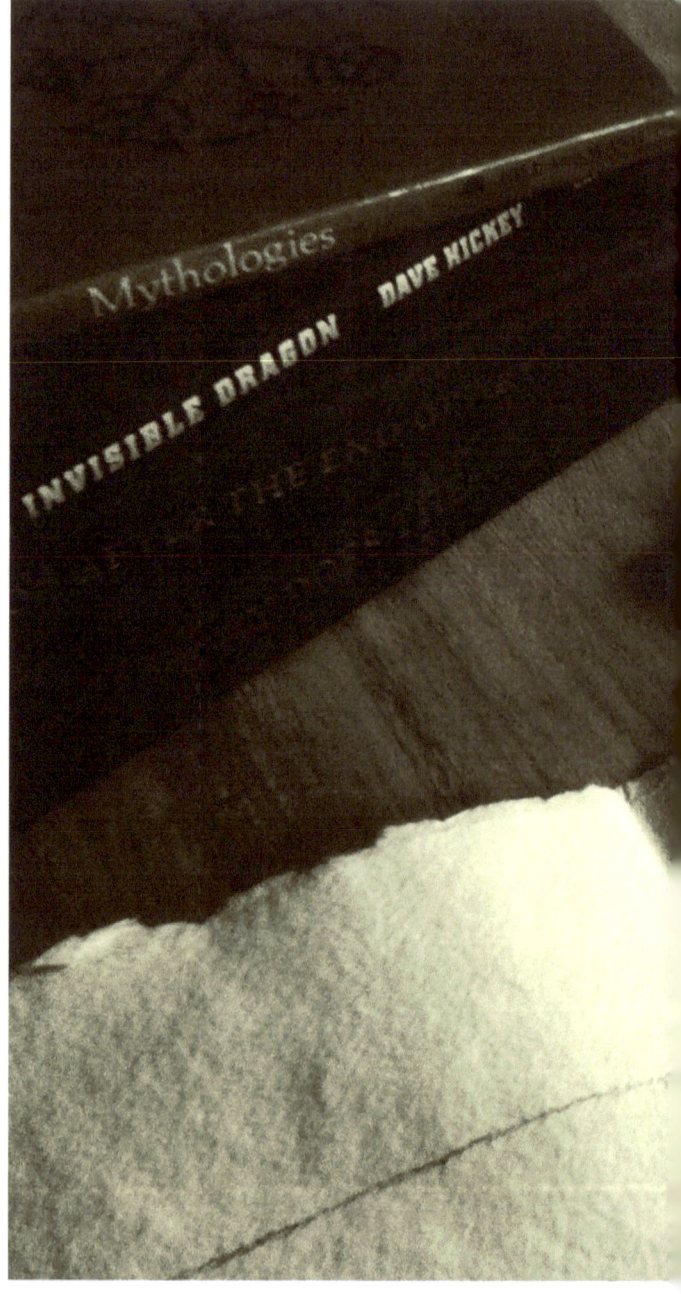

Edited and with an Introduction by Hal Foster

Contributors

11

Robin Arnold
Midnight Sun, 2011

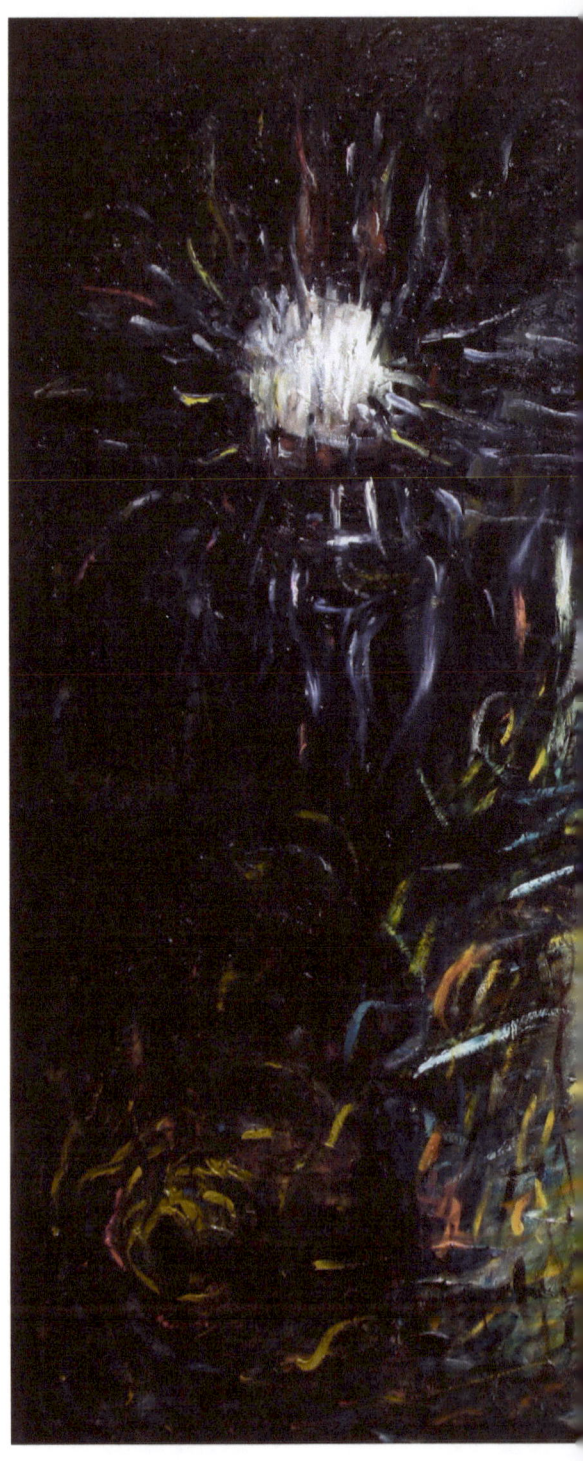

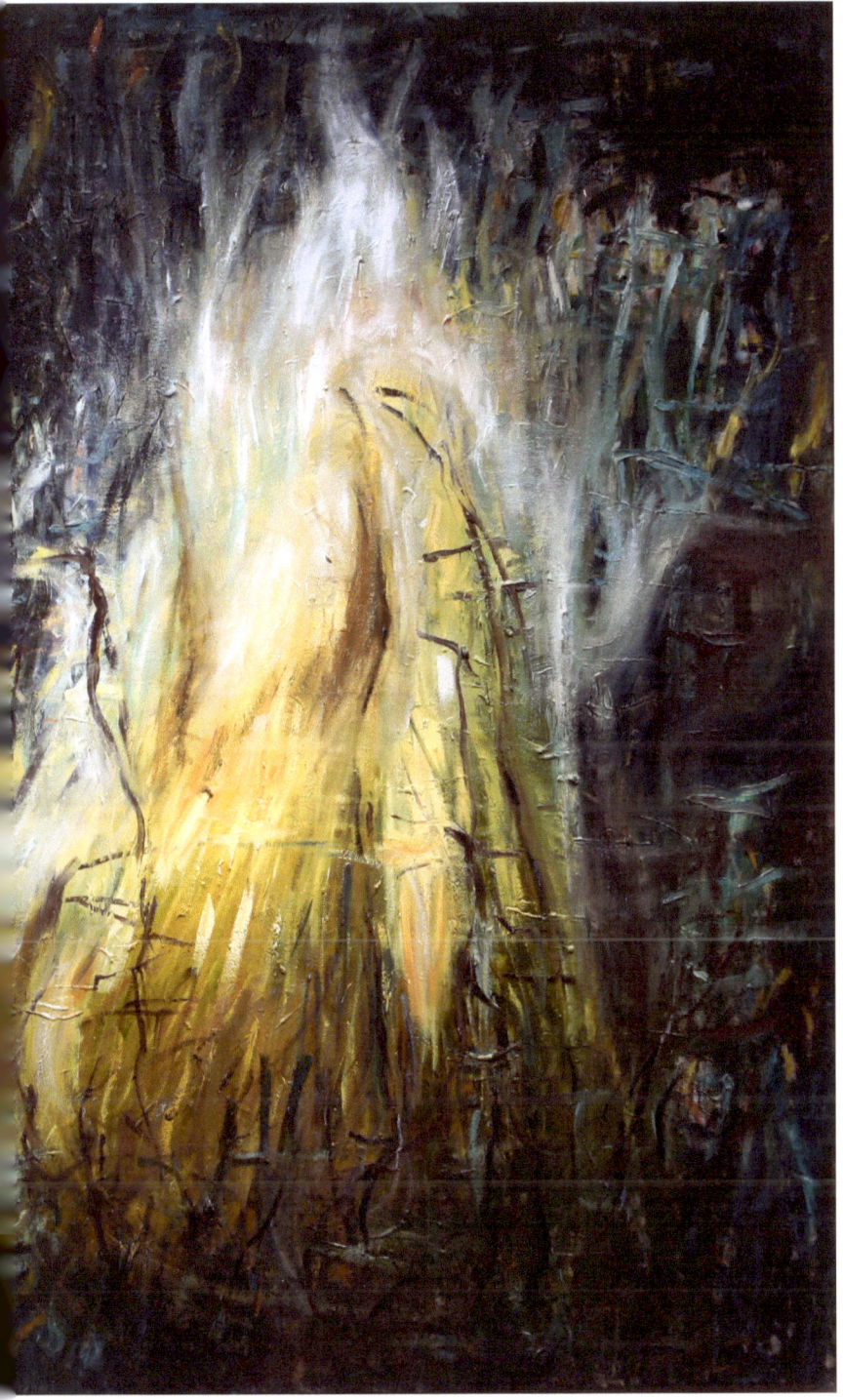

Jamie Bennett
Queste #21, Brooch, 2012

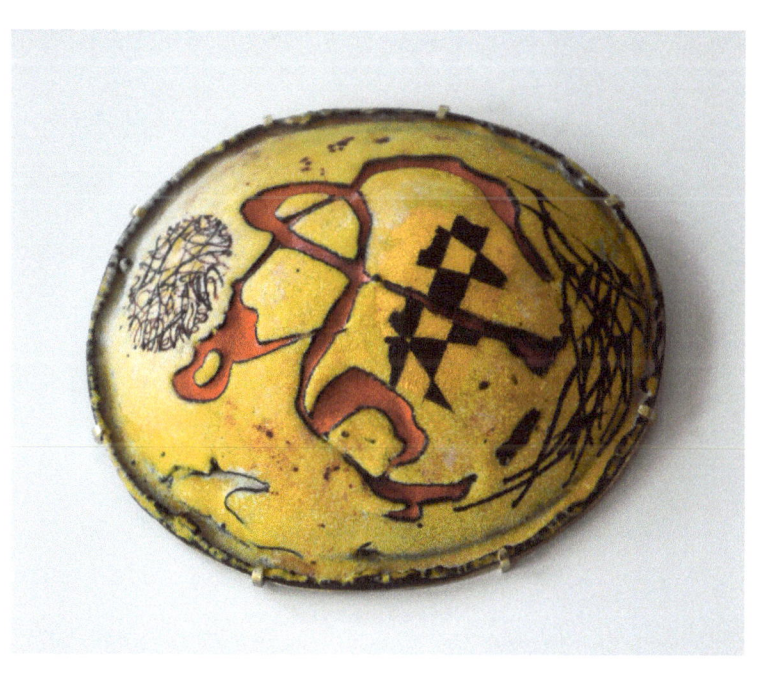

Steven P. Bradford
Survival, 2012
Dead Man Shoes, 2007

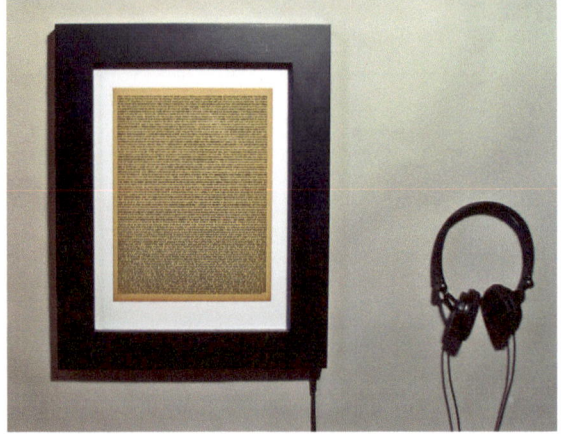

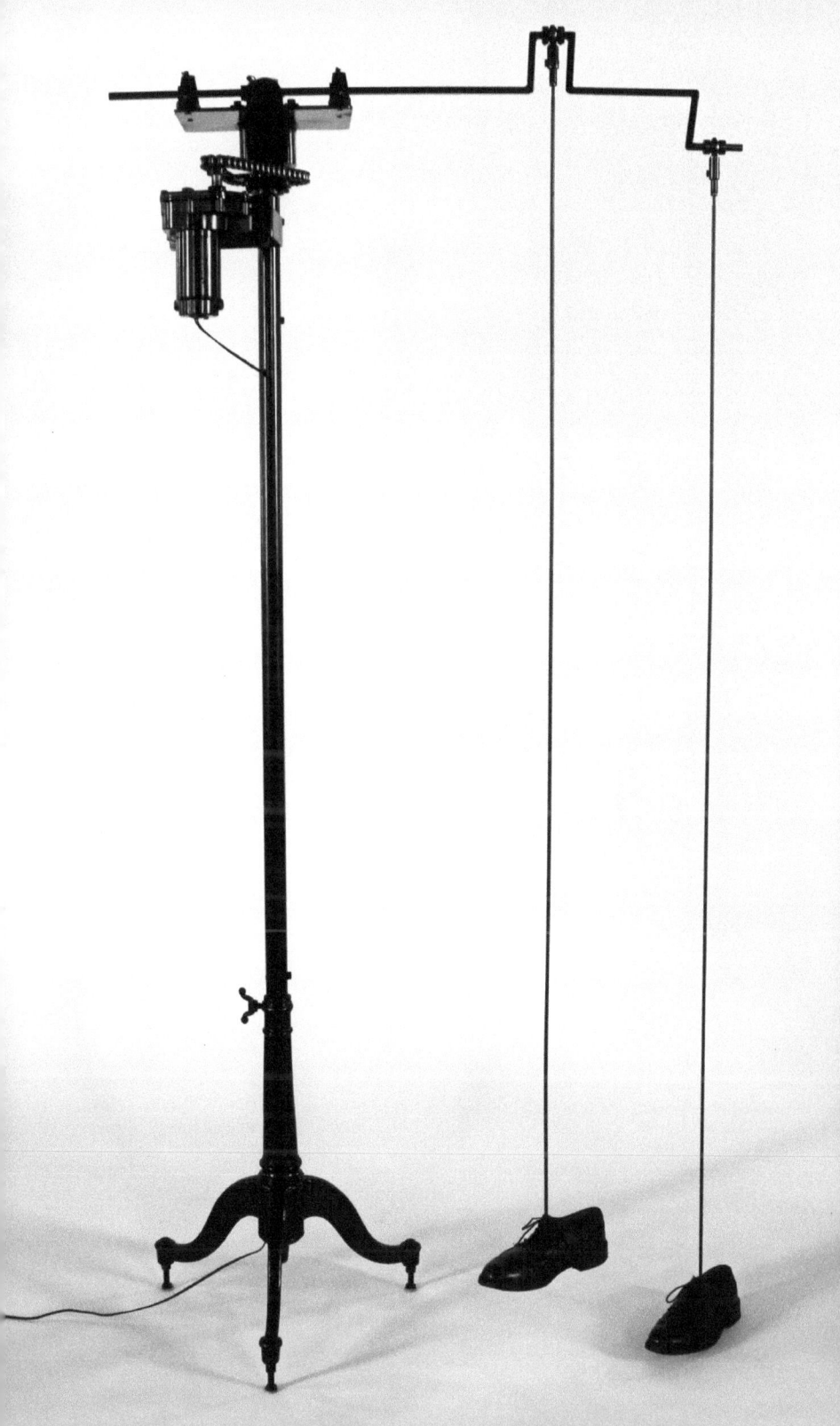

Rimer Cardillo

Gus and Pond Reflections II, from the series *From the* Estancias *to the Hudson Valley,* 2009

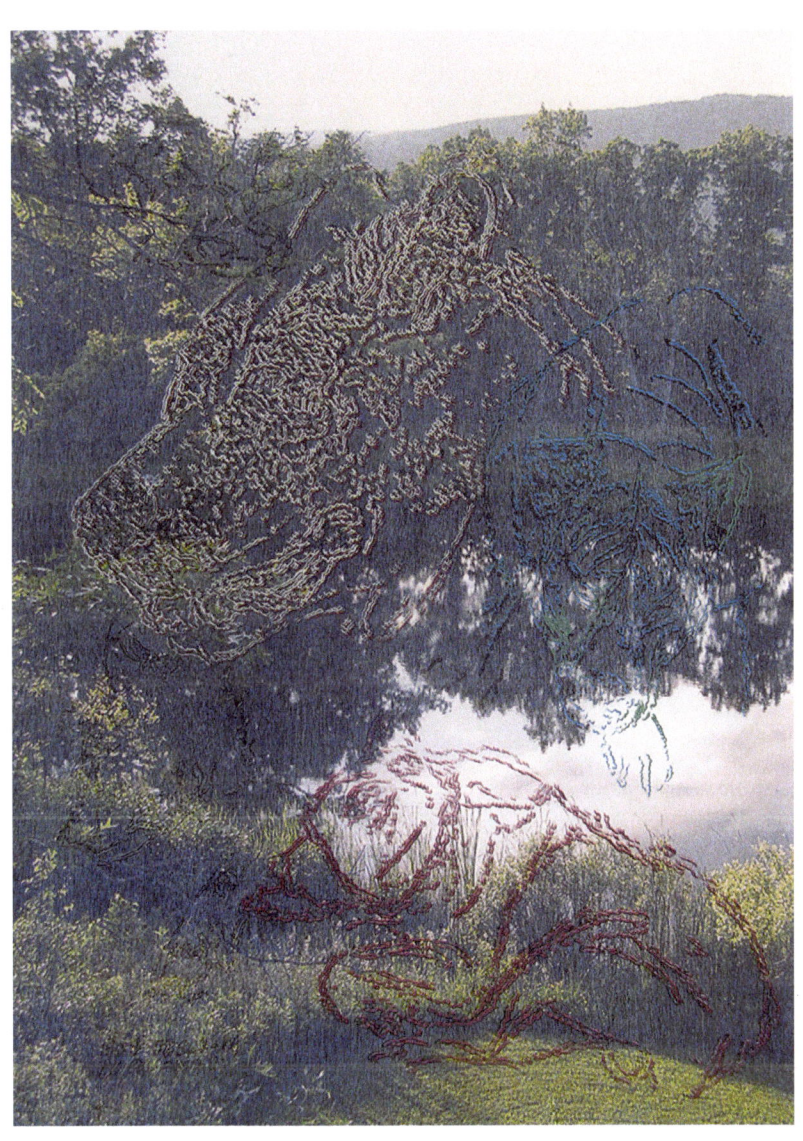

Amy Cheng

Topkapi, 2011
Broaching the Subject, 2012

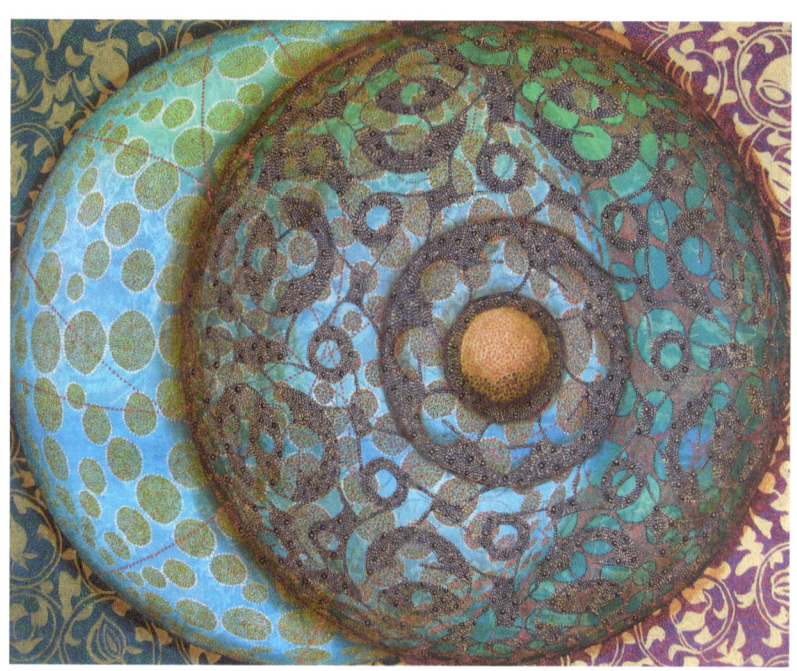

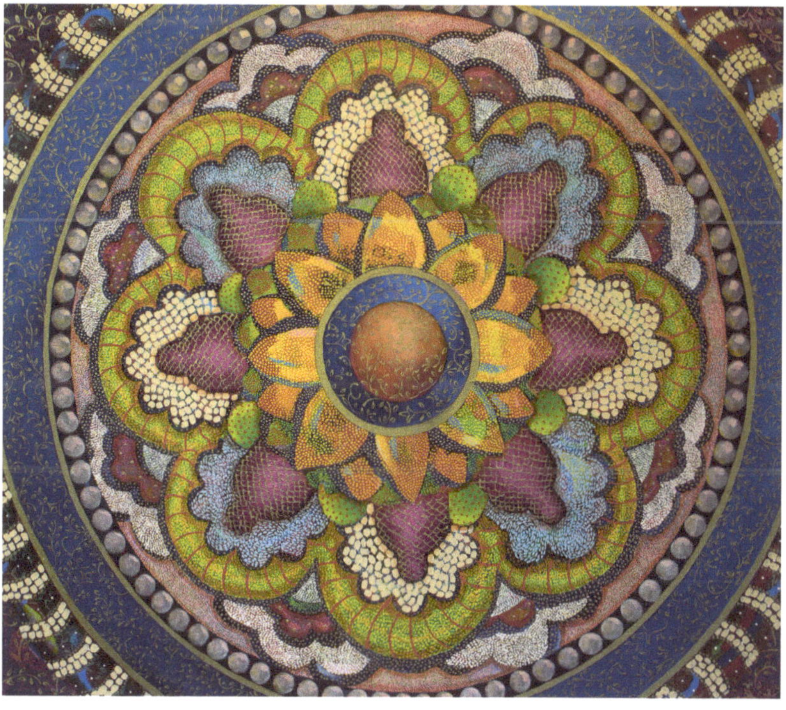

Bryan Czibesz

Prototype: Wheel (Platonic, Production, Consumable, and Iconic Forms), 2011–13

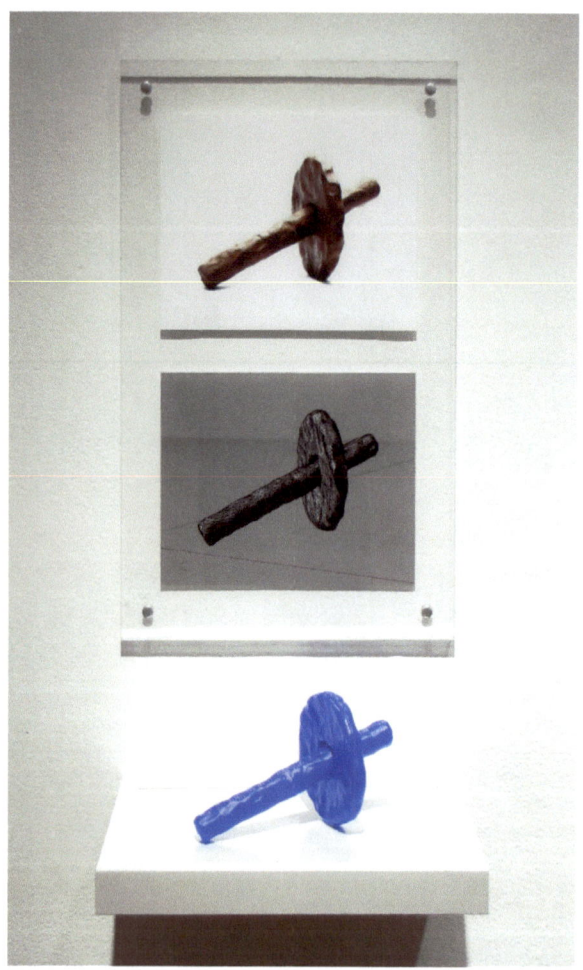

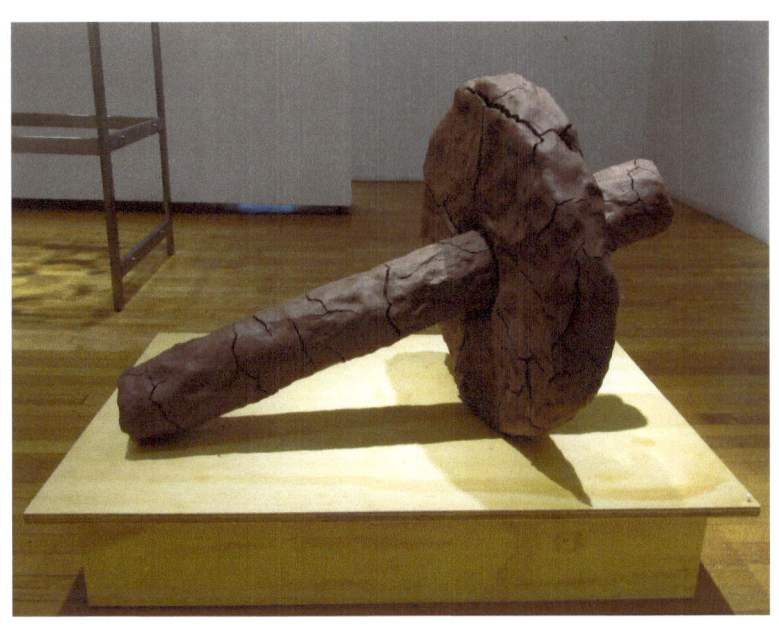

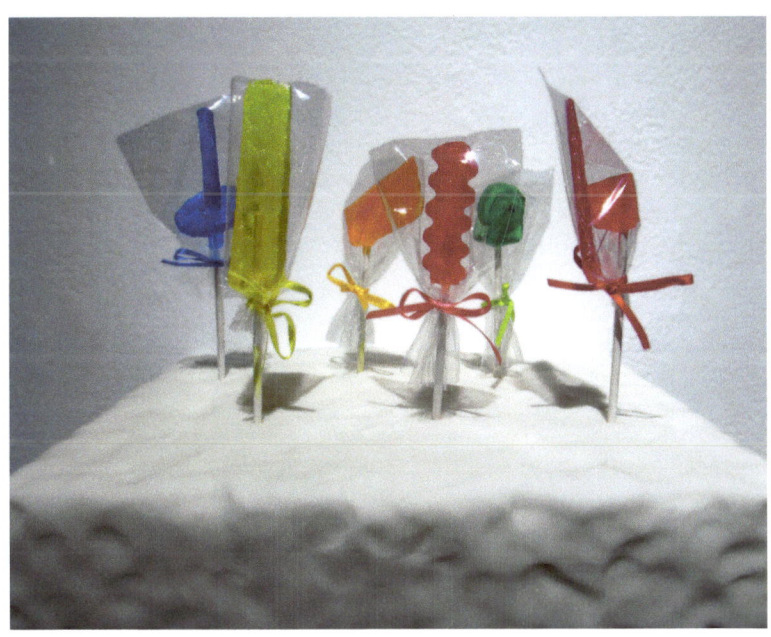

François Deschamps

Colonial Hat, from the series *Absence of Presence*, 2007

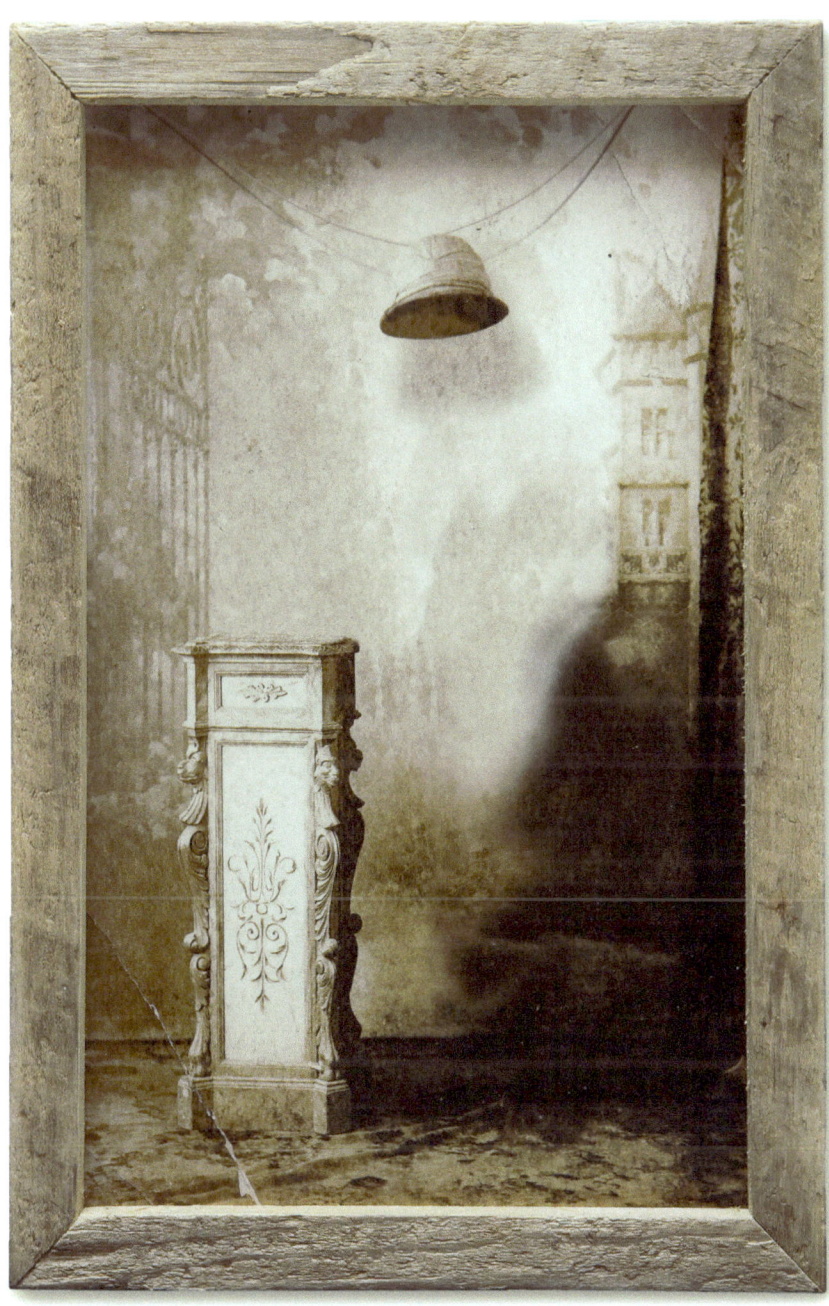

James Fossett
Three Women, 2011

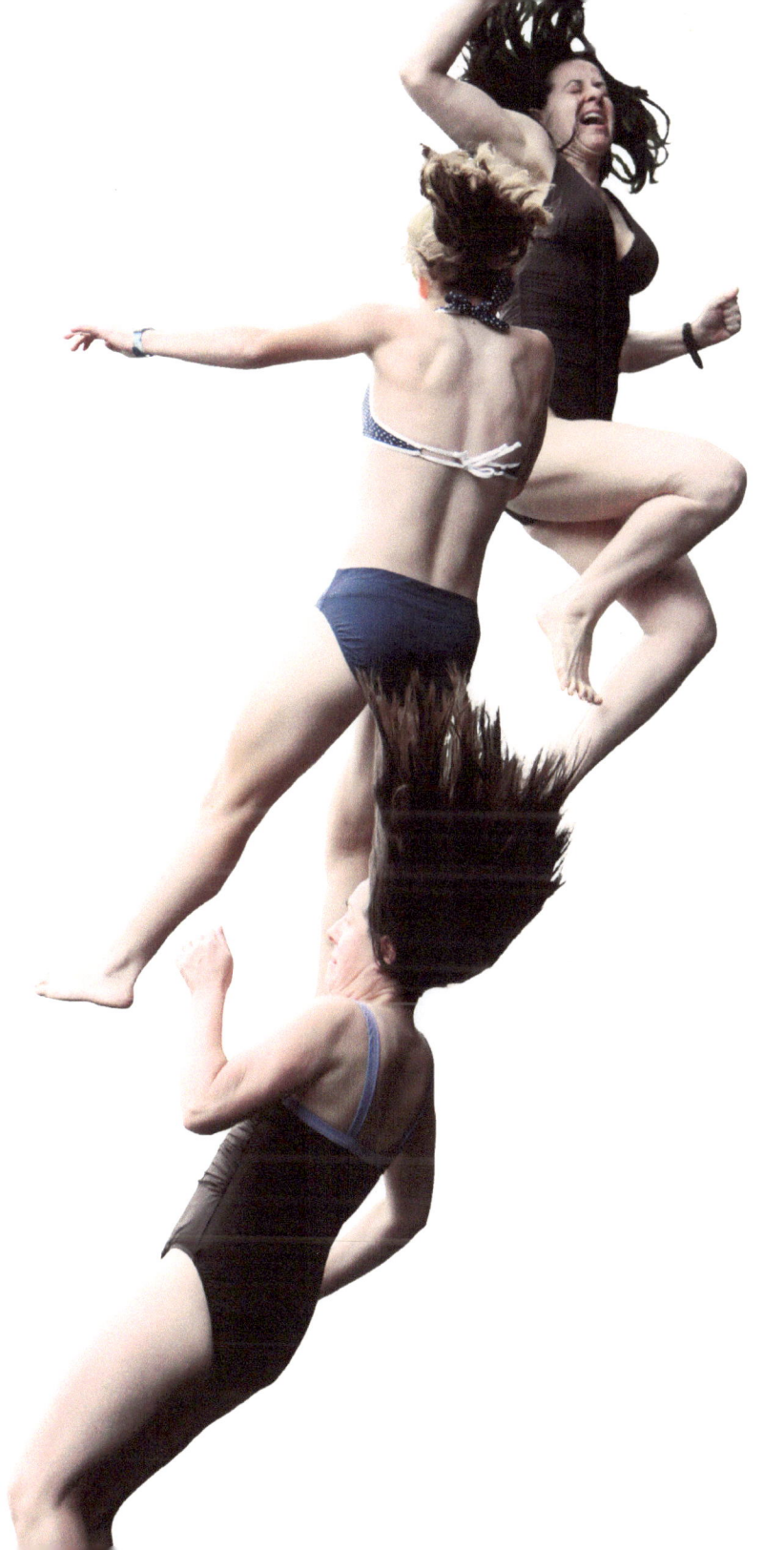

Andrea Frank

Plant #1, 2012
Classroom #3, 2011
Classroom #4, 2011
Classroom #8, 2011

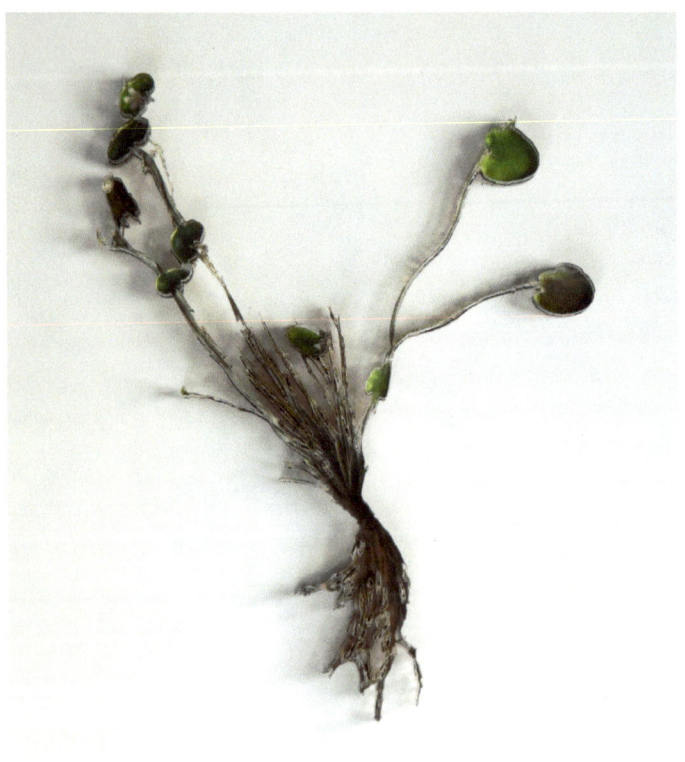

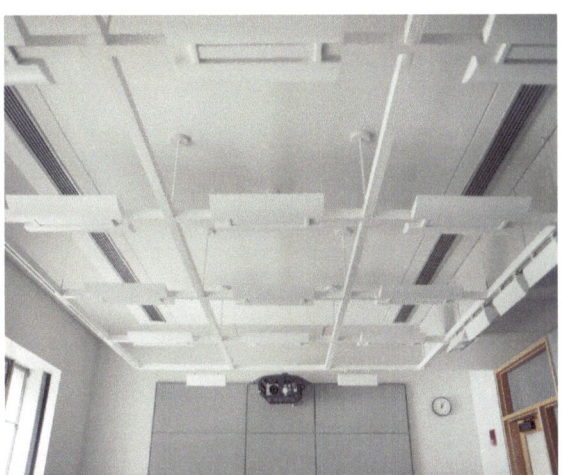

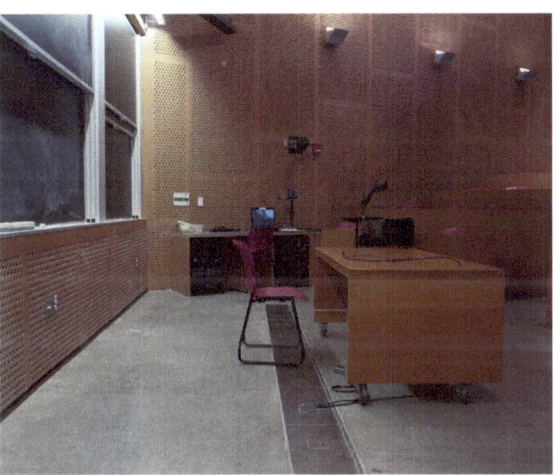

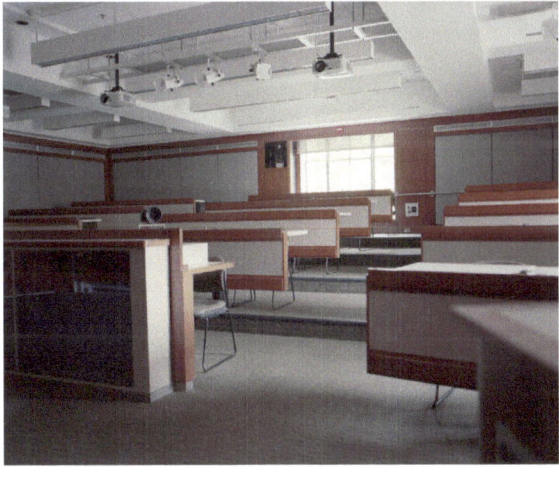

Matthew Friday

A Map Without Boundaries,
2009–ongoing

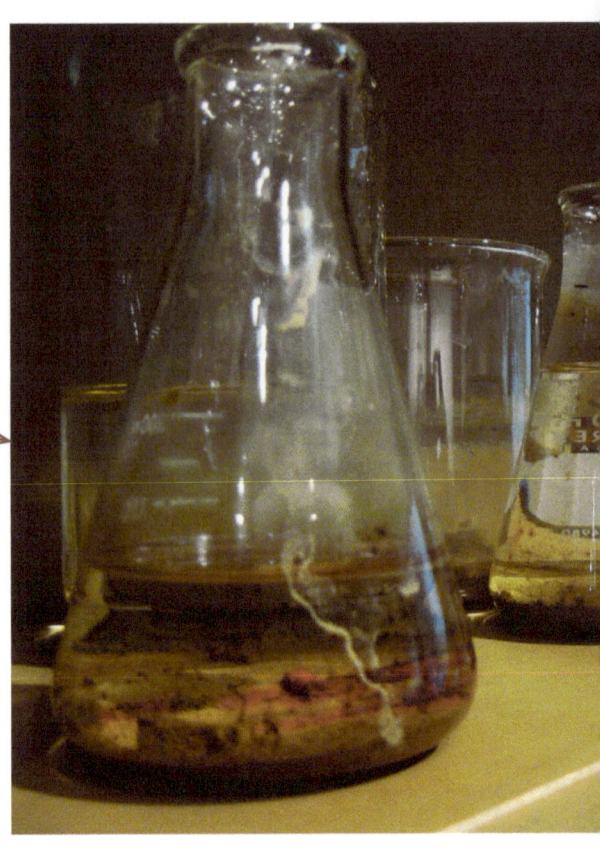

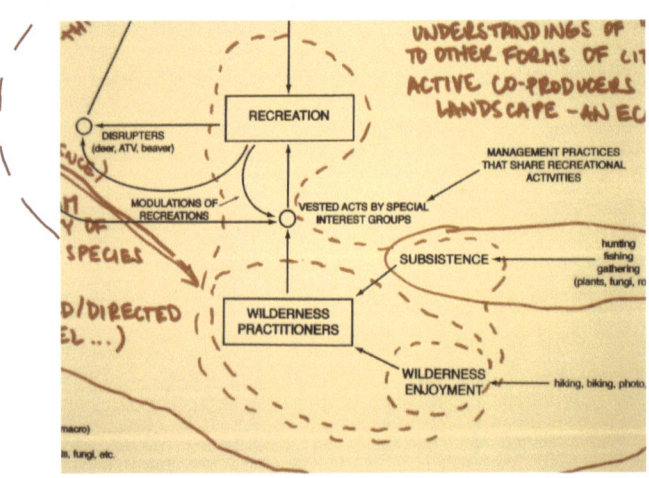

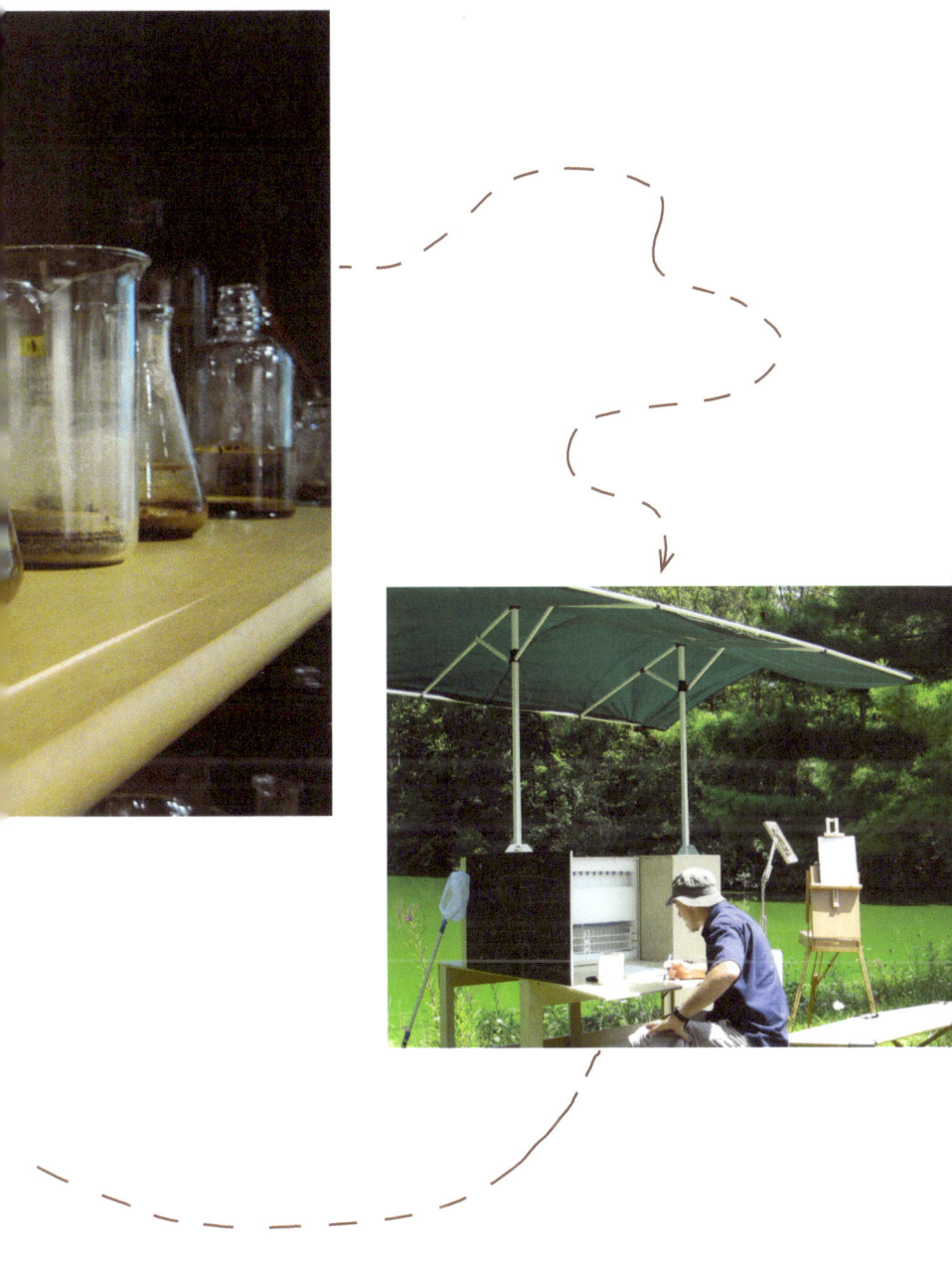

Kathy Goodell

Oculus Maw, 2012

Mesmer Oculus 7, 2012

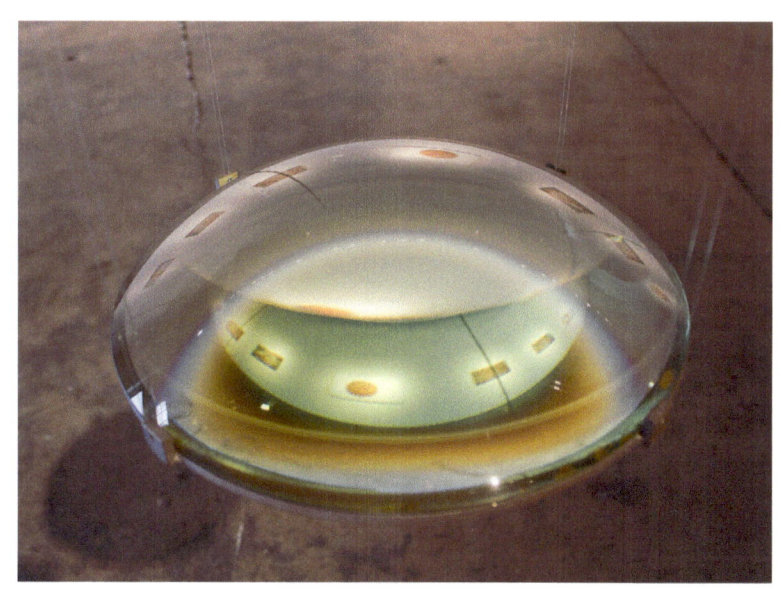

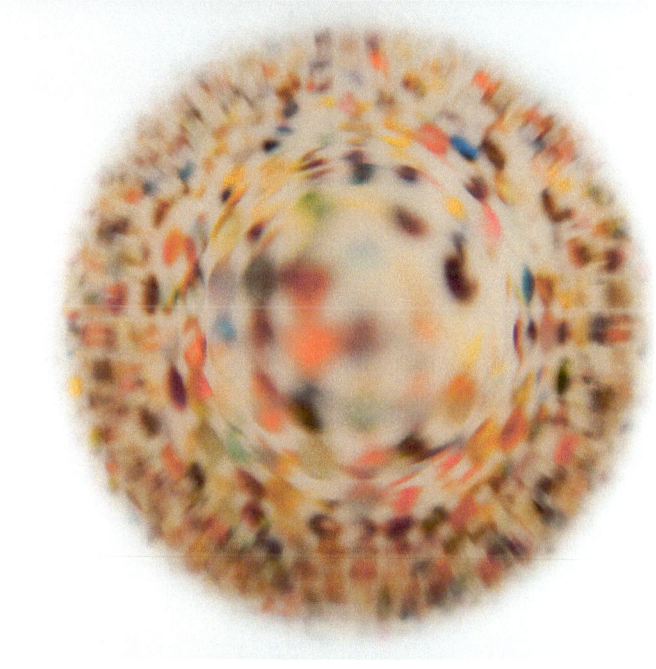

Rena Leinberger

Utopias, Unmoored, 2012

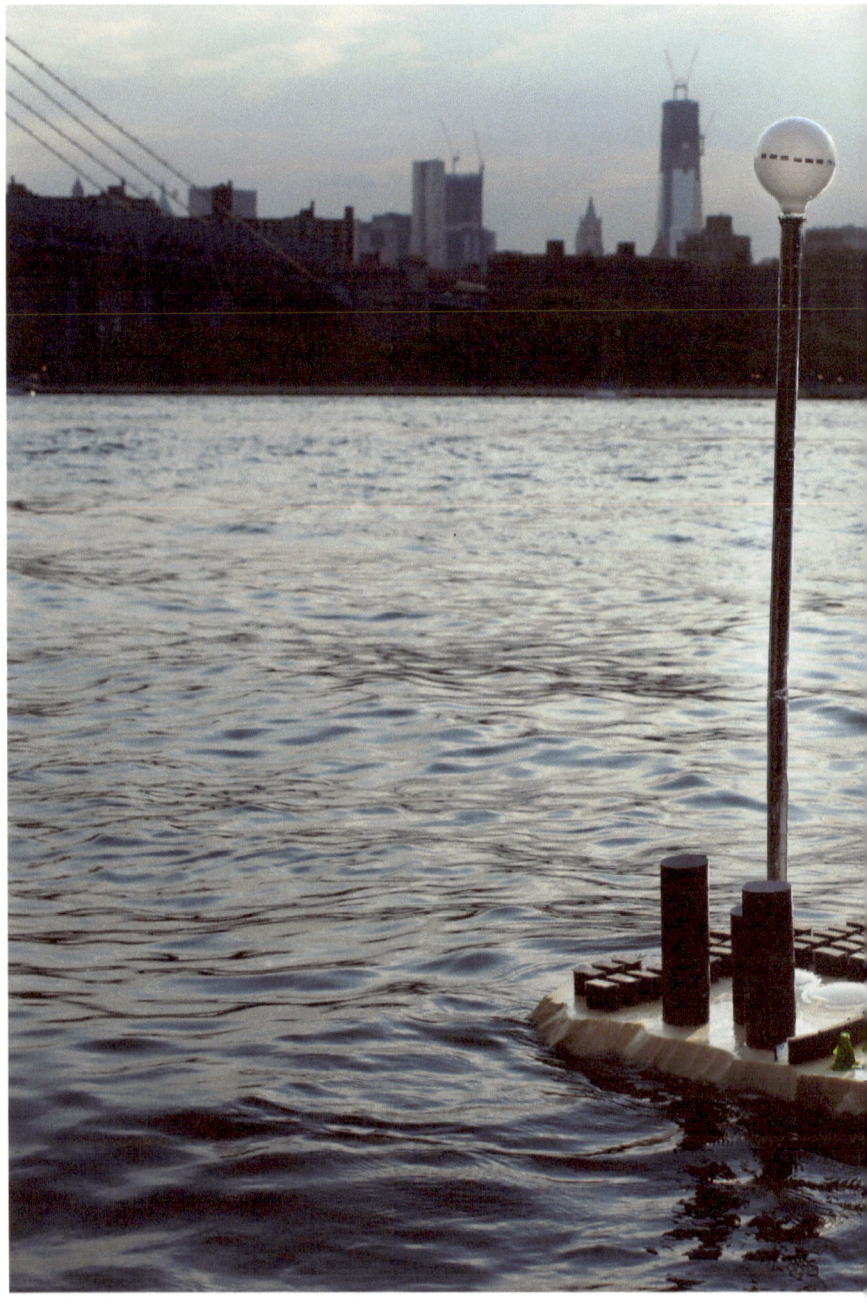

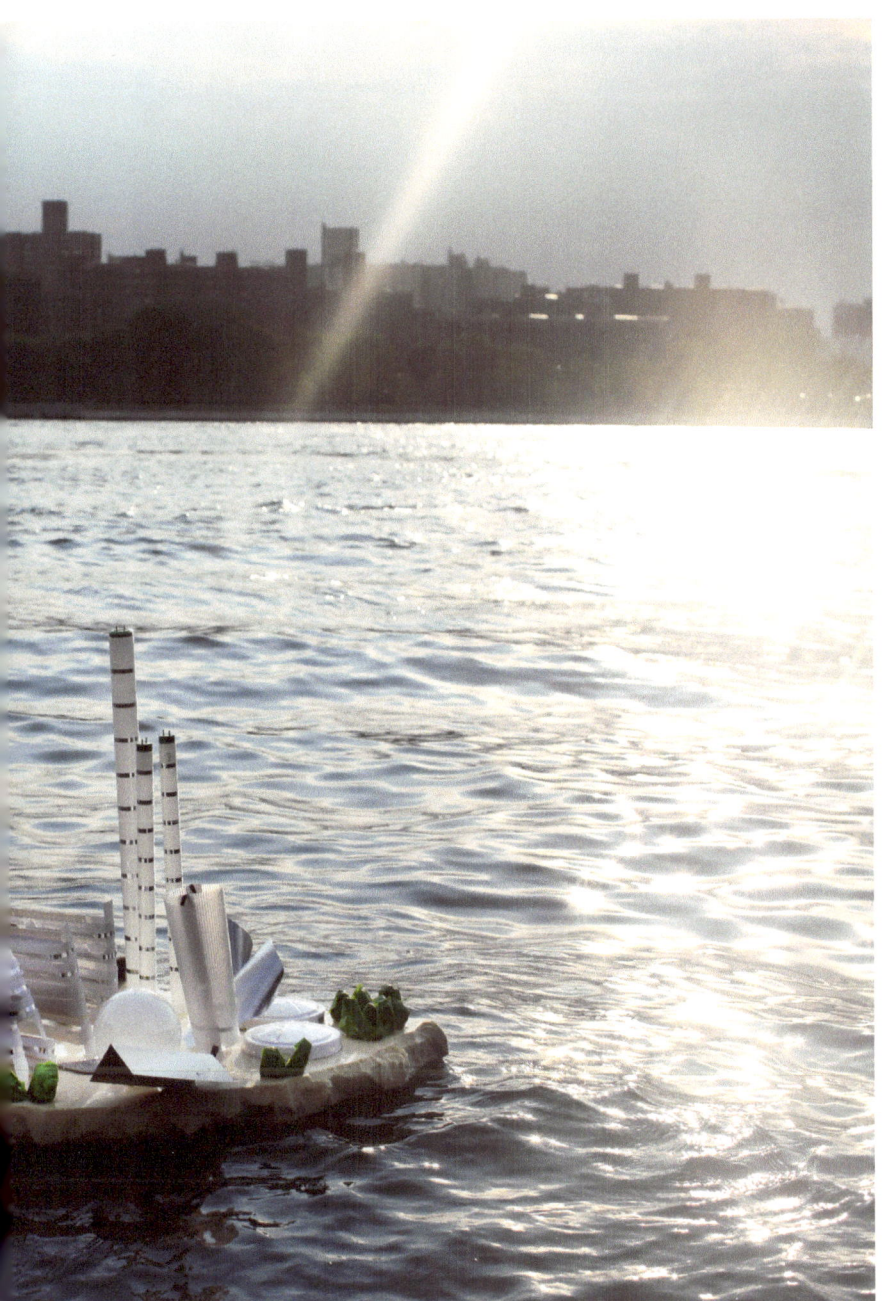

Carmen Lizardo

Equivalent #1, from the series *Equivalent #1 to #12*, 2013

Ann Lovett
Untitled (Sisters, Oregon), 2012
Untitled (Kerlingarfjöll, Iceland), 2011

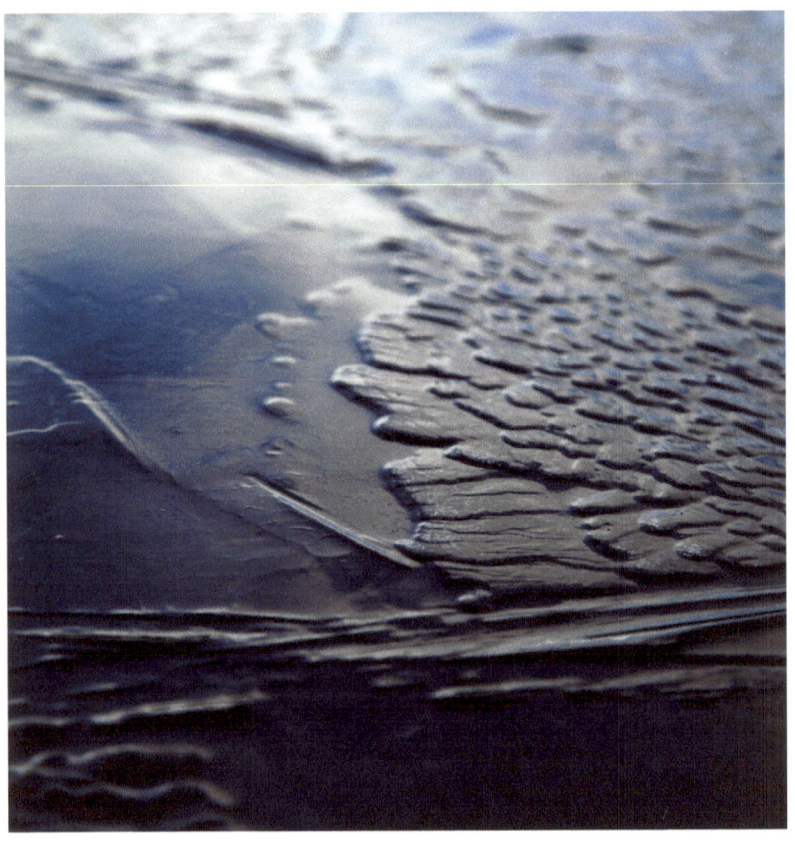

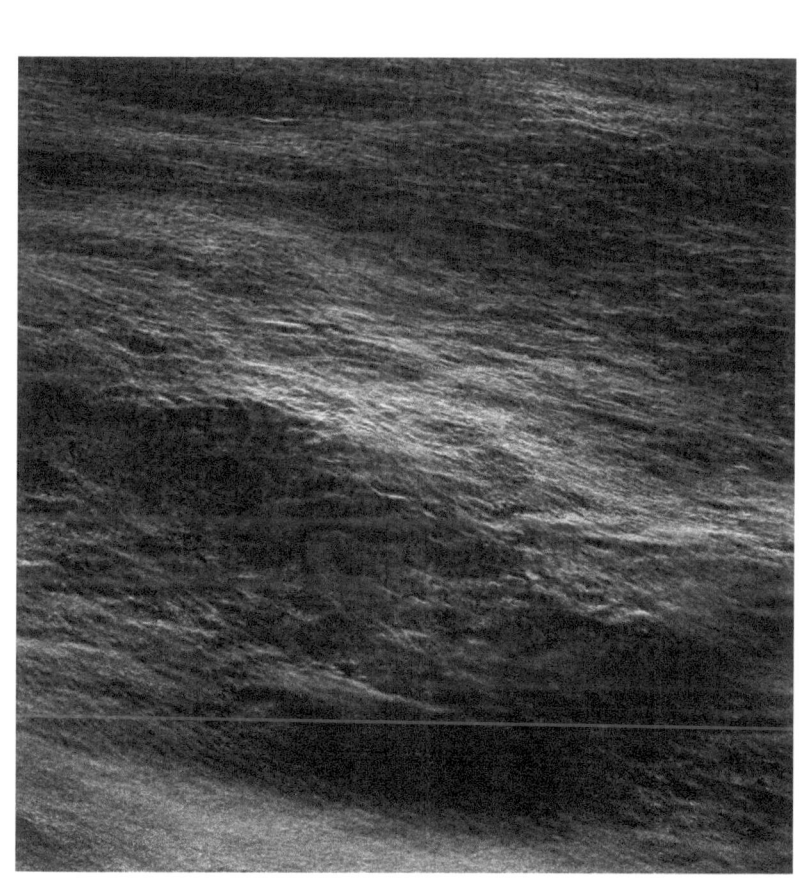

Aleánna Luethi·Garrecht

Lineform and Letterform: Typography in Textural Experiences, June 2012

Type History

press

«

ink

paper

hand mould

platen

matrix

alloy

ñ lead

antimony

Aa

Aa

Aa

Aa

Aa

æ

7 8 9

4 5 6 7

1 2 3 0

& ? @ ff

ct ß Ħ O

ct

&

tin

tempering

frisket

counter

punch

Myra Mimlitsch-Gray

Wooden, 2007
Clove Oval, 2010

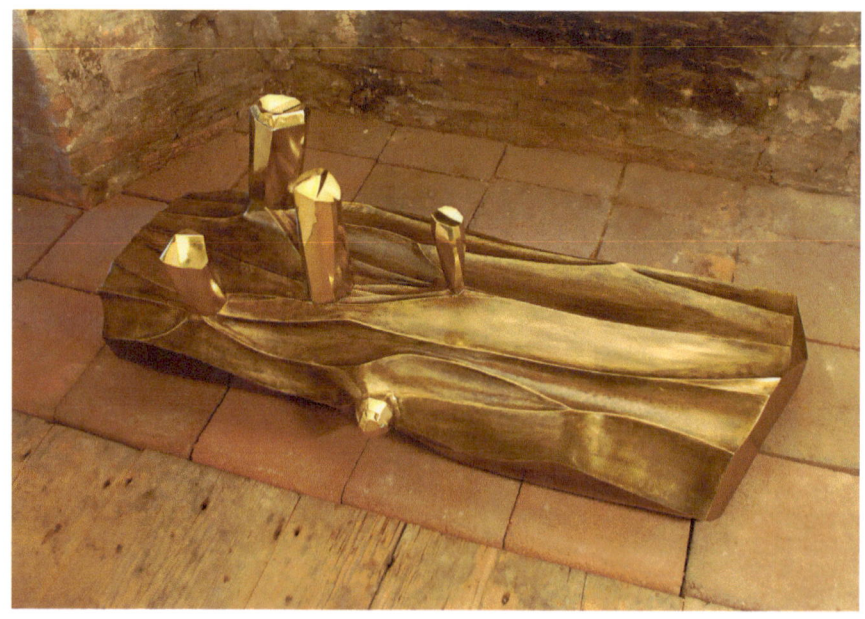

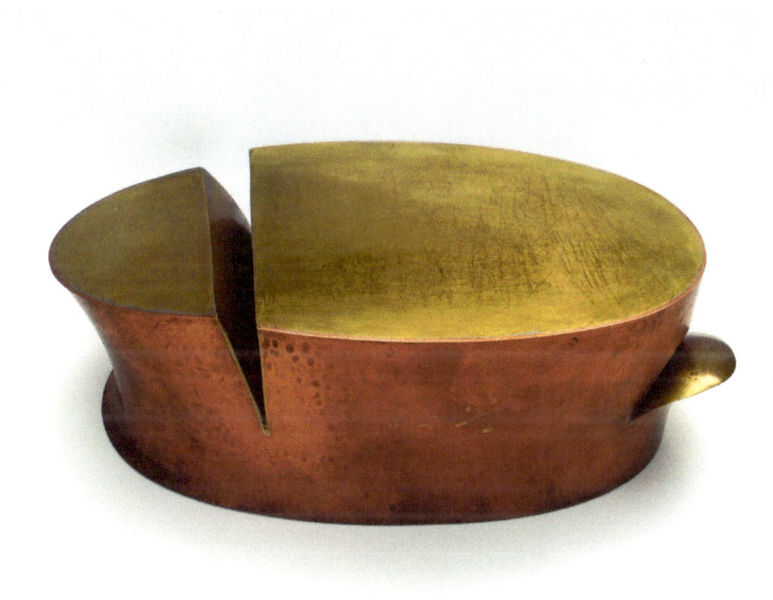

Itty S. Neuhaus
Scratch Berg, 2011

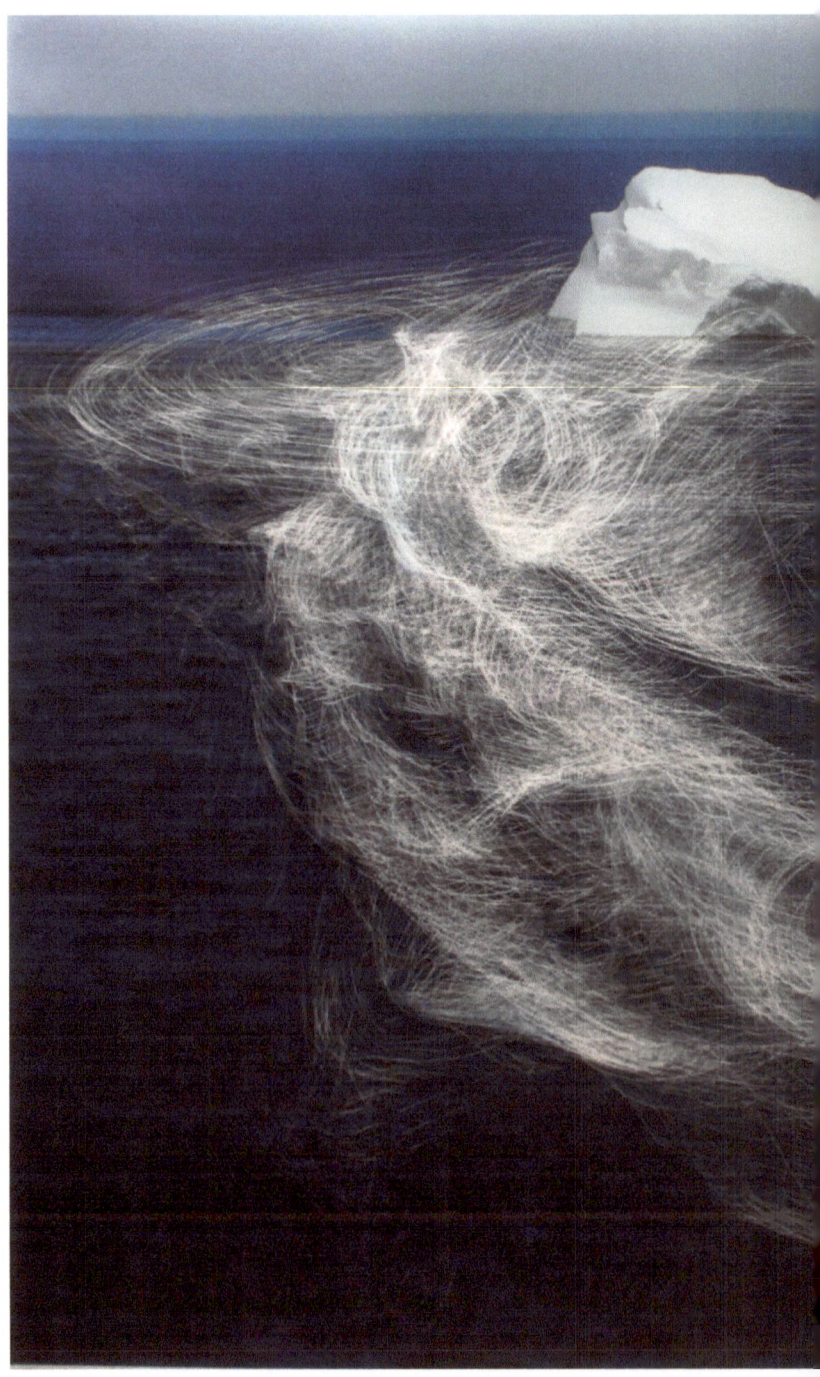

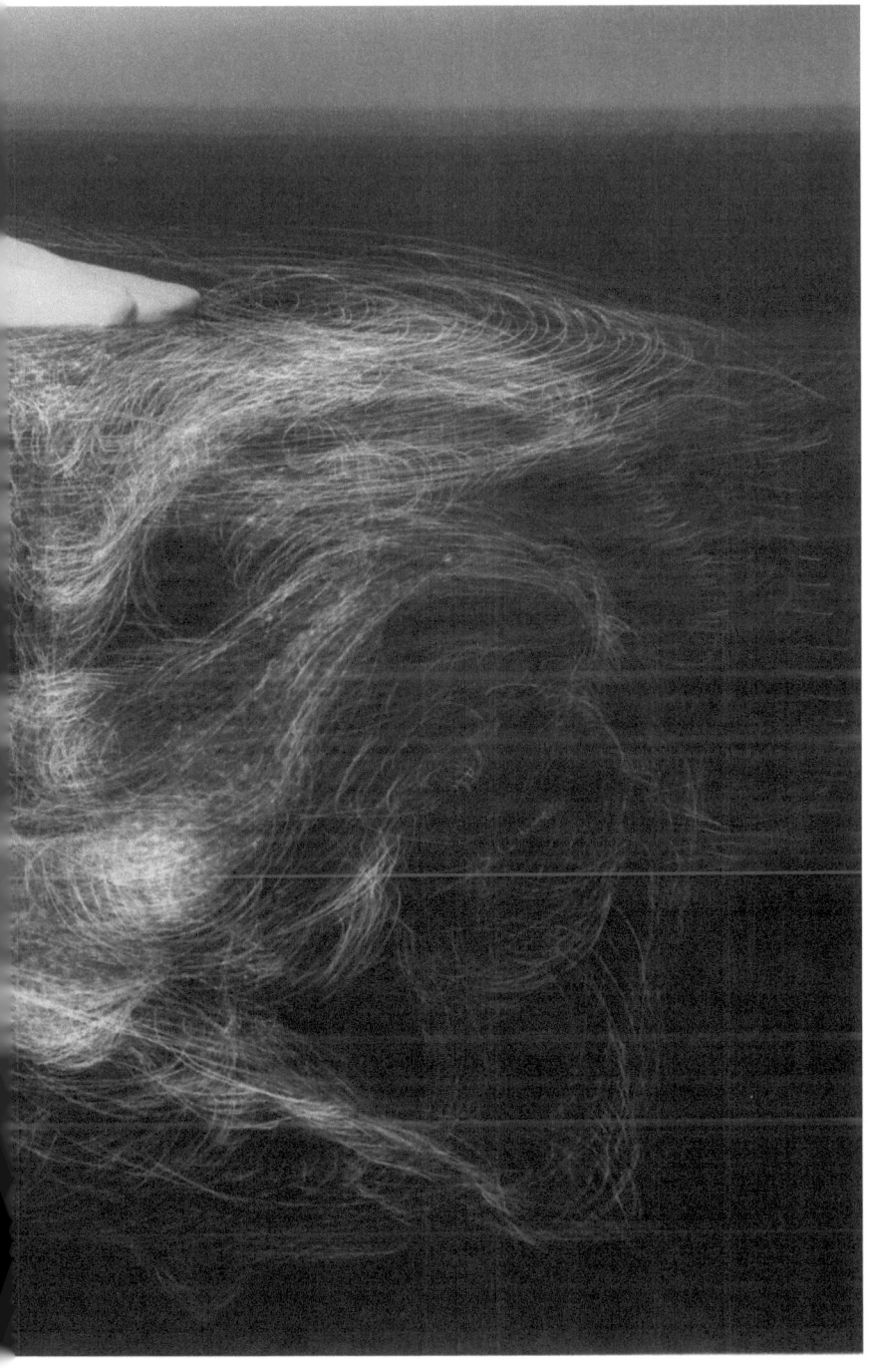

Amy Papaelias
PersonaType: Living Type Specimens, 2012

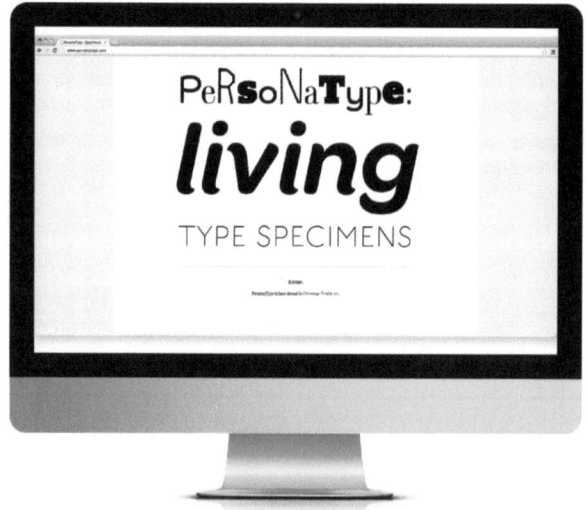

PeRsoNaTYpe:
living
TYPE SPECIMENS

/ select a persona /

Happy
Emotional
Friendly
Stressed
Excited
Masculine
Feminine

/ participate /

Lend your voice to the project
and record a type specimen!
Here's how.

/ about the project /

**PersonaType: Living Type
Specimens** is an experiment in
kinetic web typography that
makes auditory and visible the
emotive qualities of type.
Read on.

How are you feeling today?
SELECT A PERSONA
to hear and see a personatype specimen
talk and move
BASED ON THE PERSONALITY OF
the voice and typeface.

Jill Parisi
Sugarplum Pinwheel (installation detail), 2011

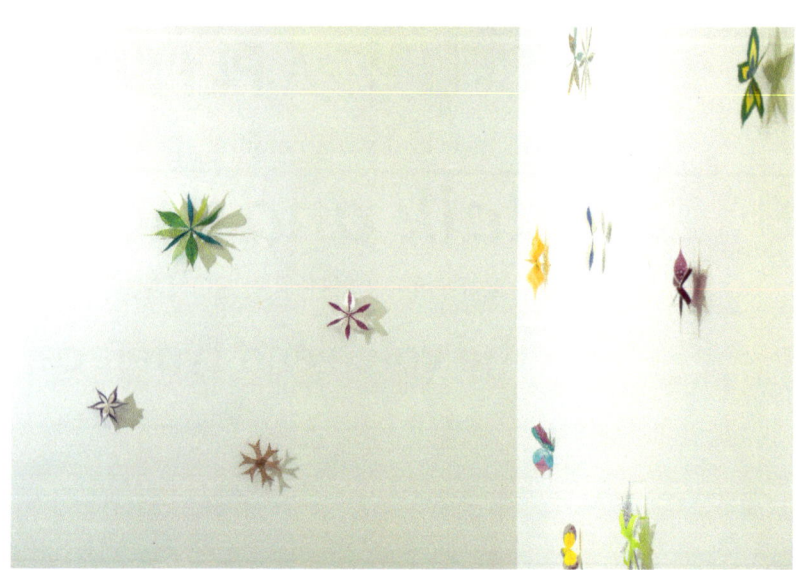

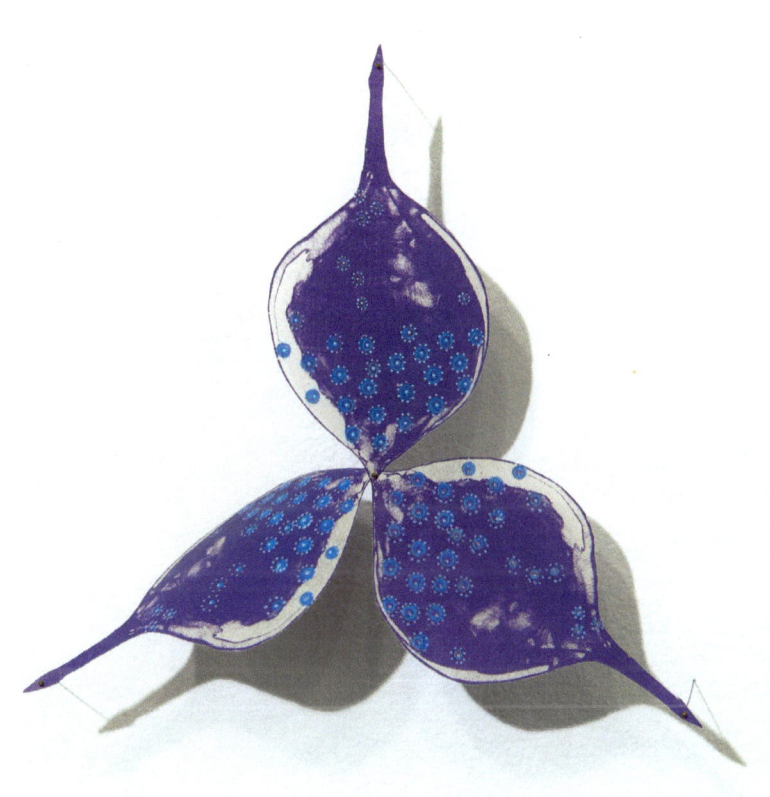

Jessica Poser

Birth of the Universe, Parts I–VI, from the series *Noise*, March 2012

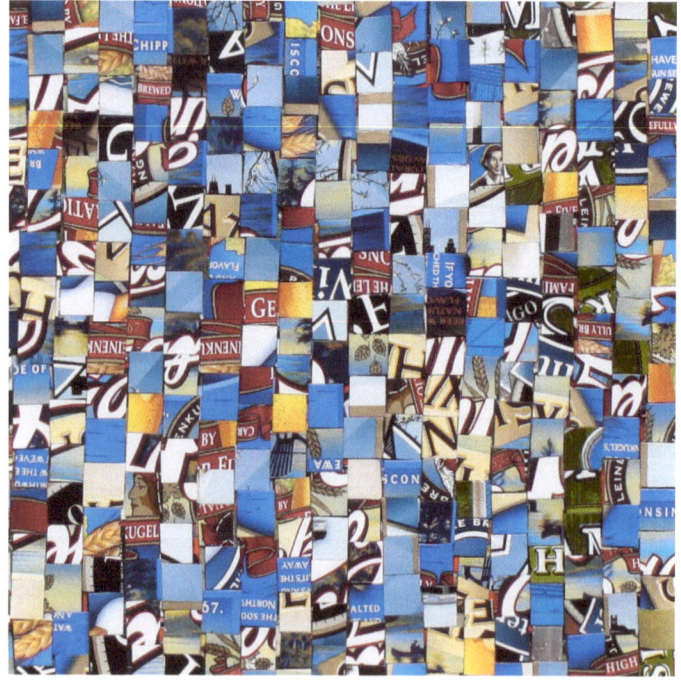

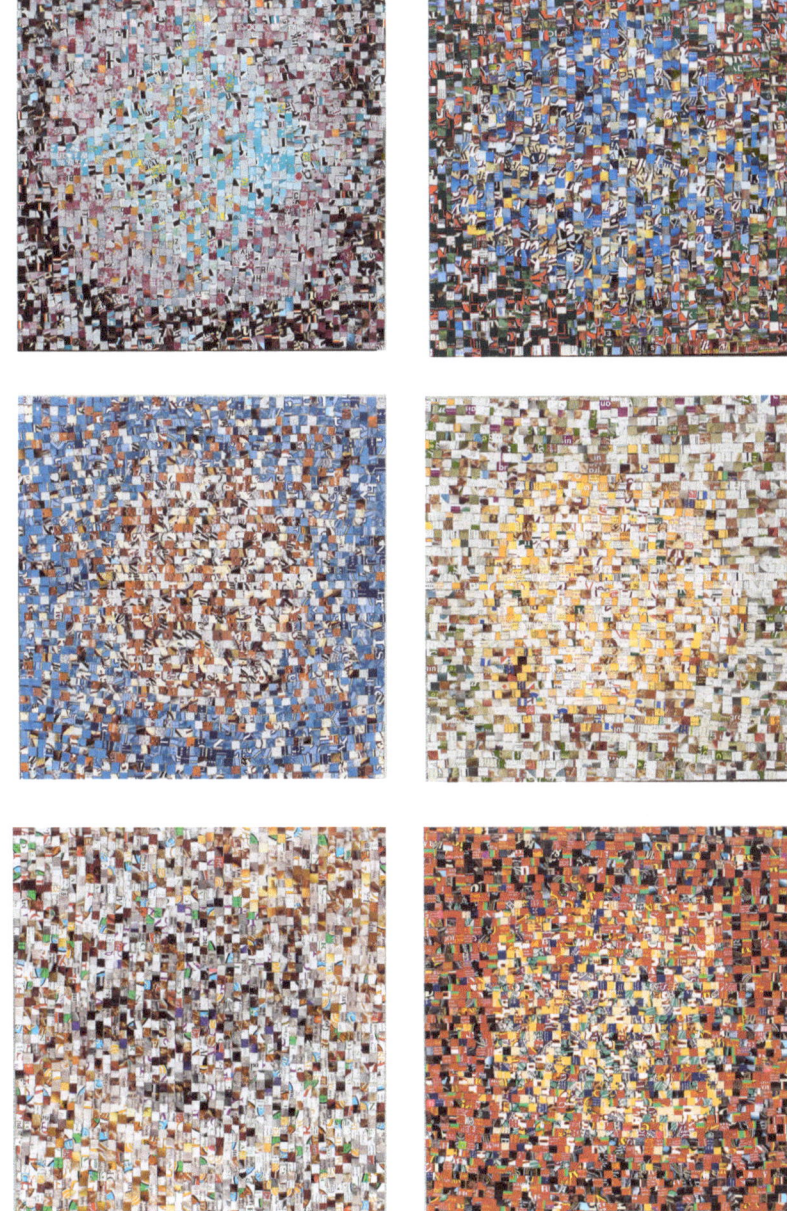

Emily Puthoff

We are floating in a medium of vast extent (excerpt from Pascal's *Pensées*), 2007–2013

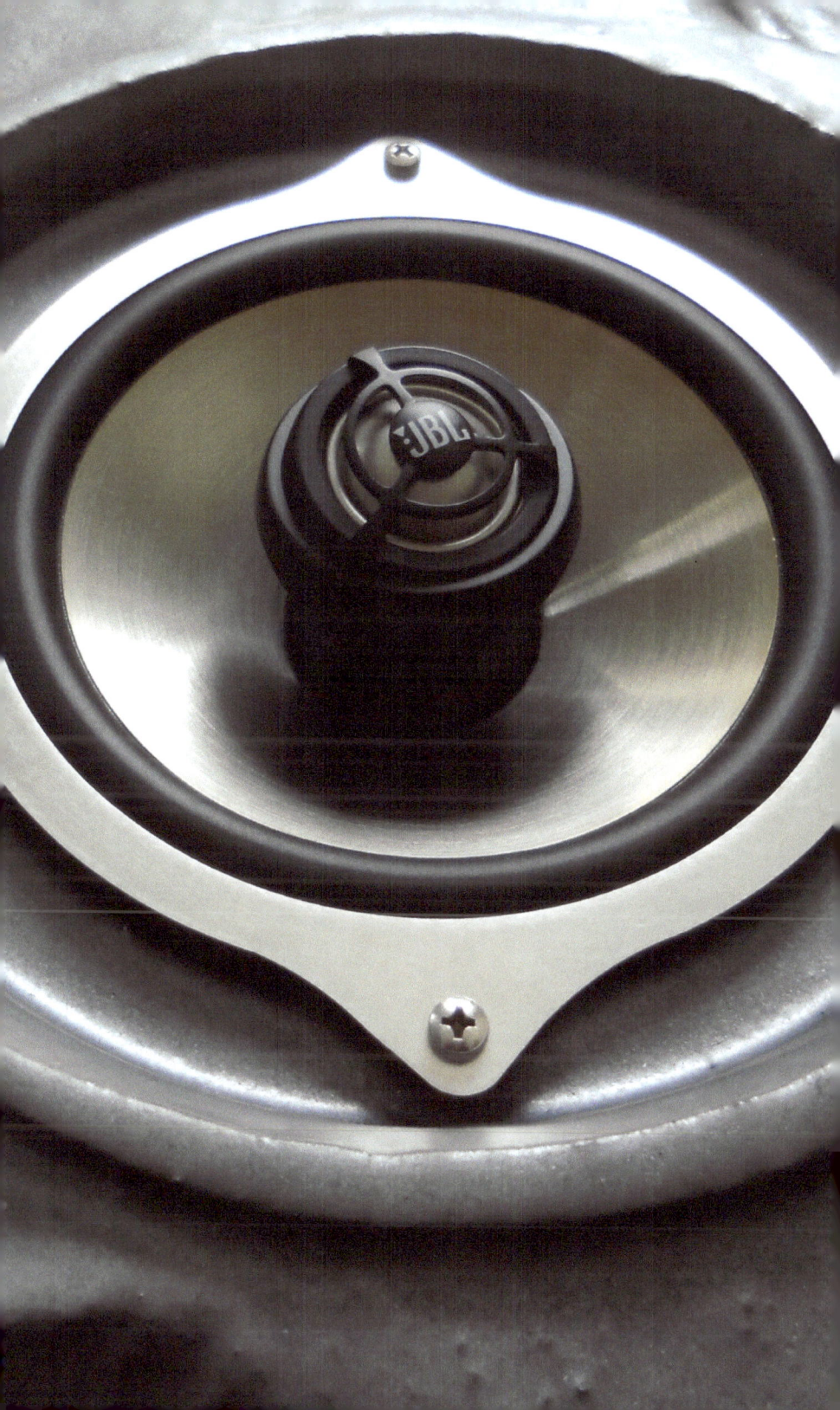

Thomas Sarrantonio
Swarm, 2012

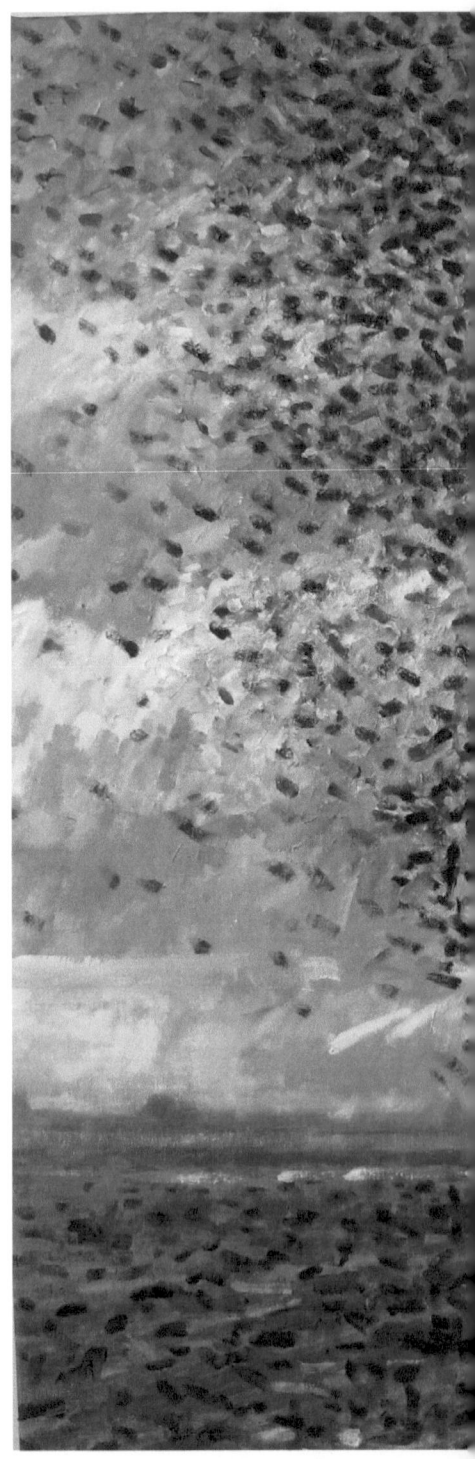

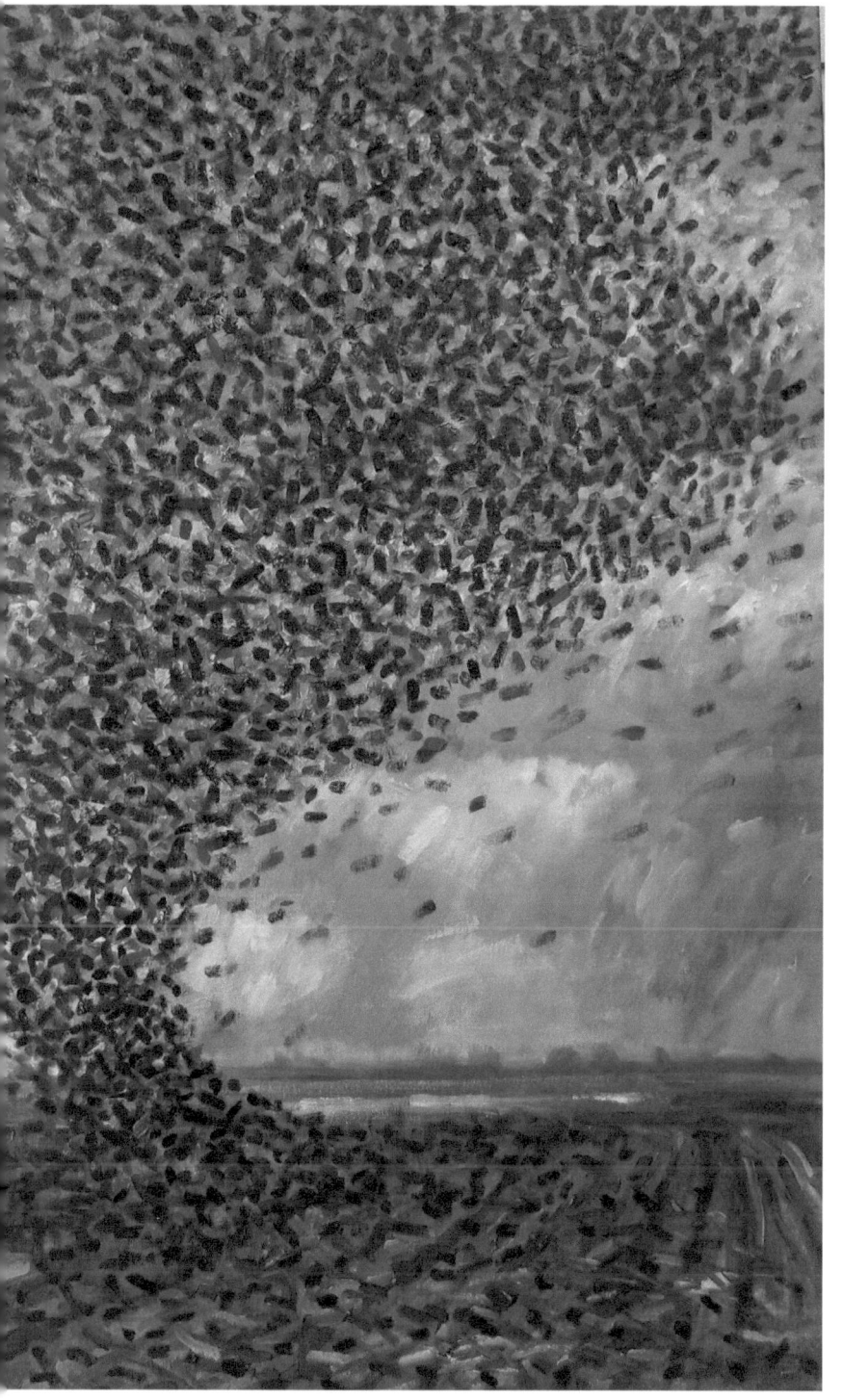

Anat Shiftan
Garden Views, 2012

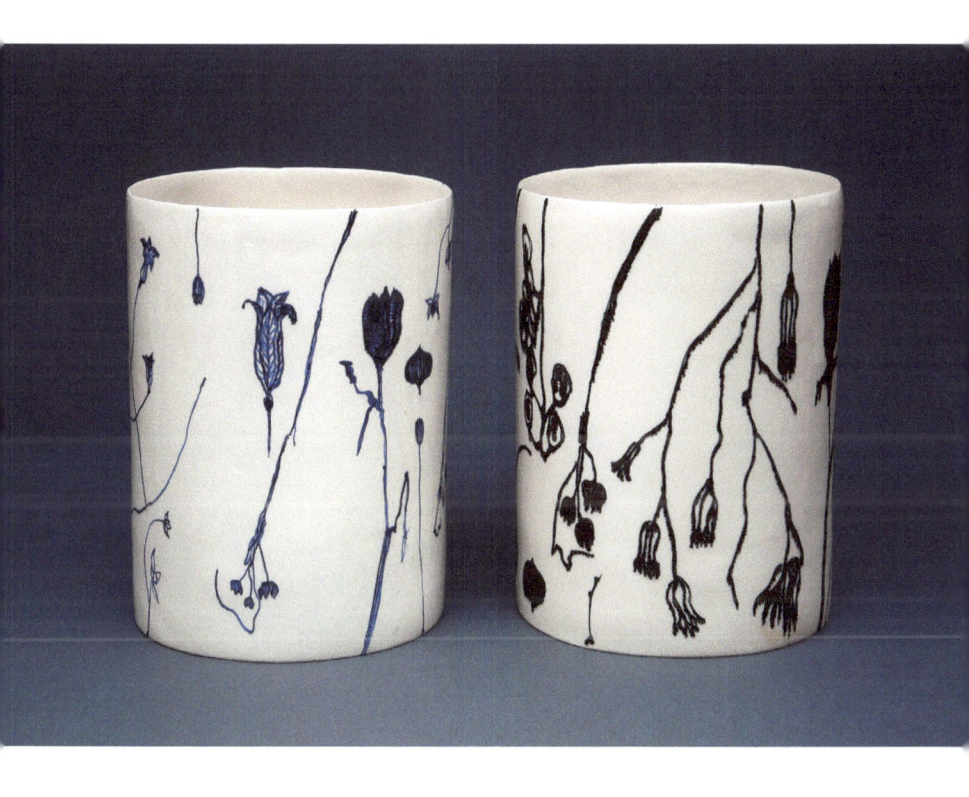

Suzanne Stokes
Ascension, 2012

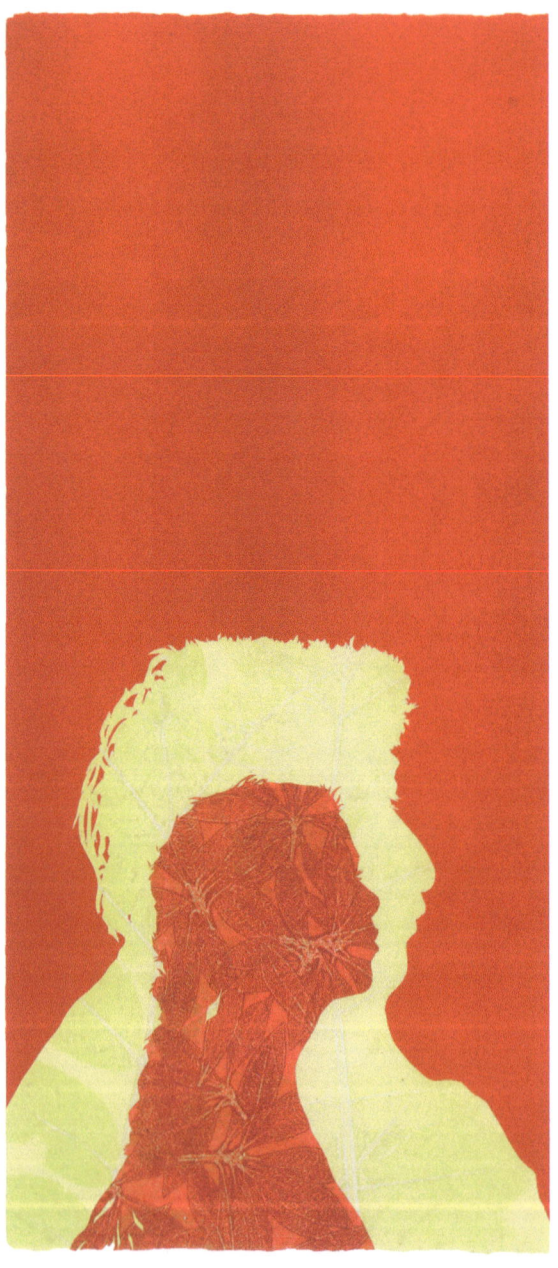

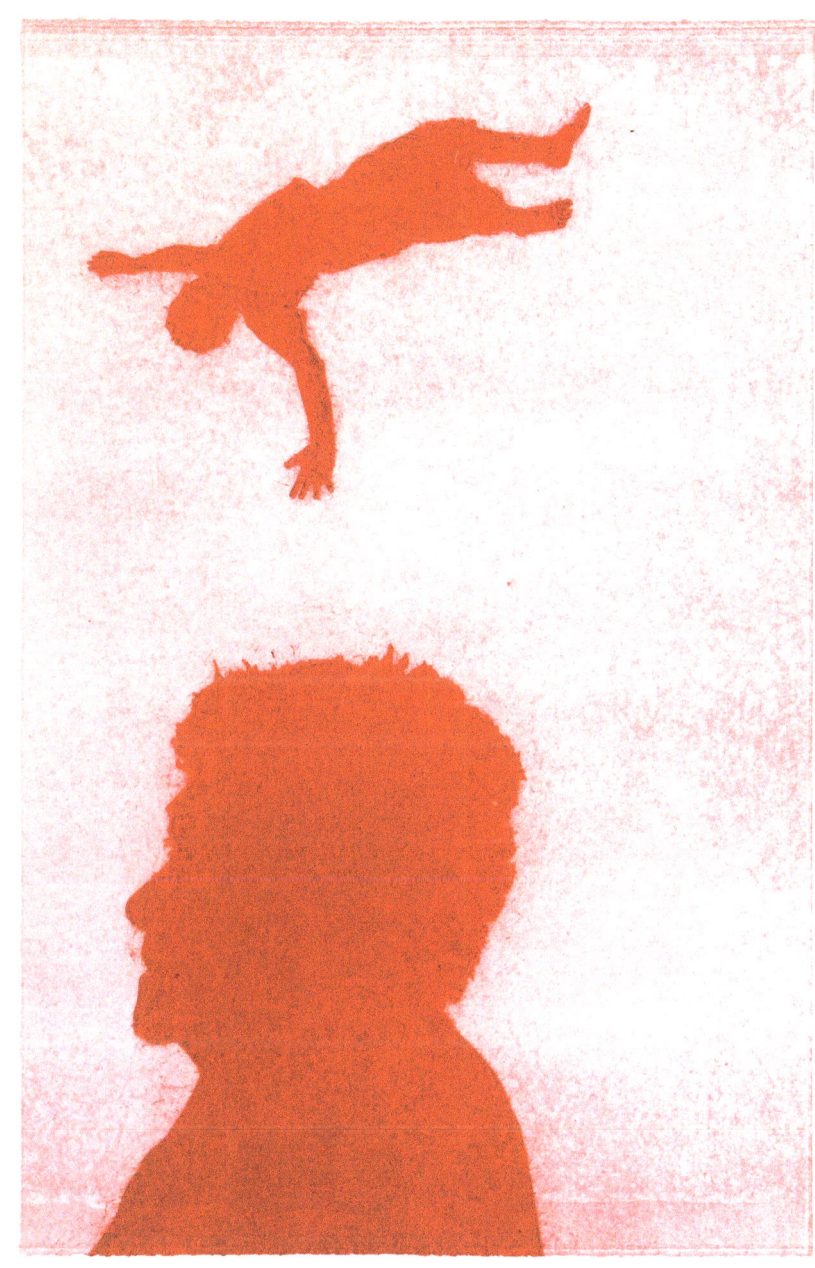

Alice Wexler
Charlie 1, June 2012

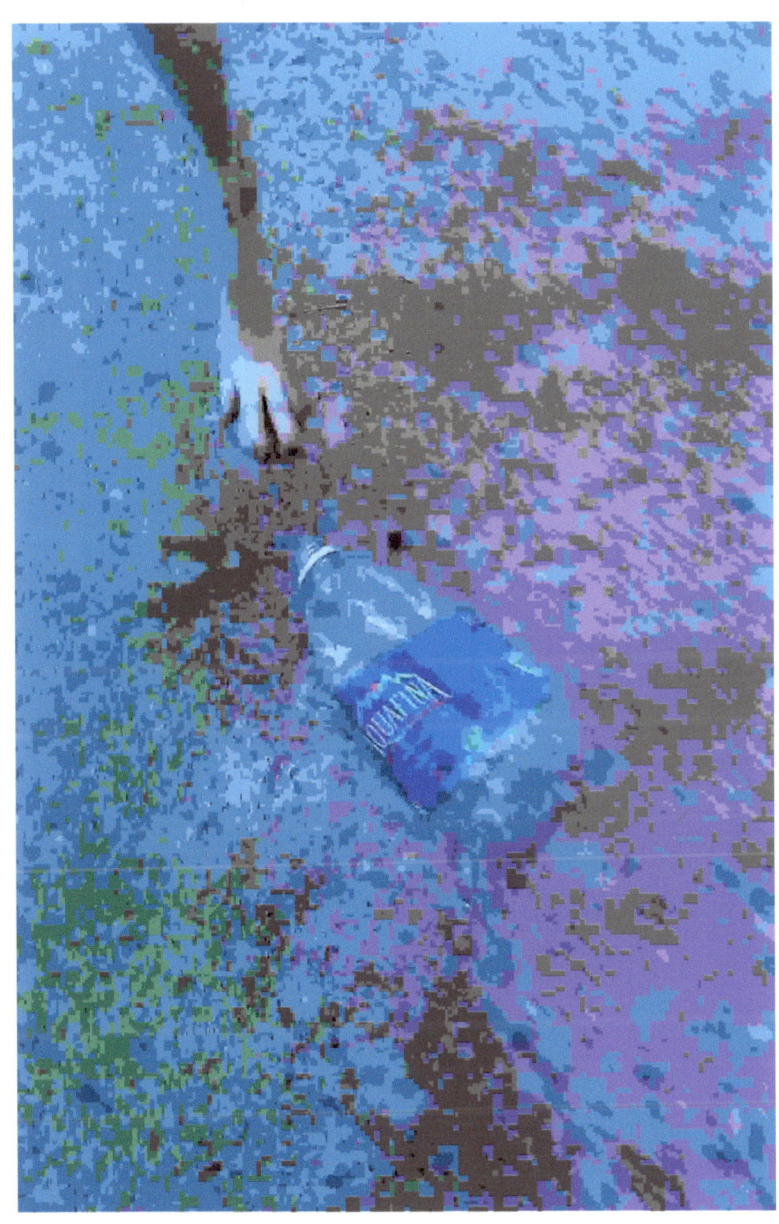

Cheryl Wheat
Hypnerotomachia, 2012

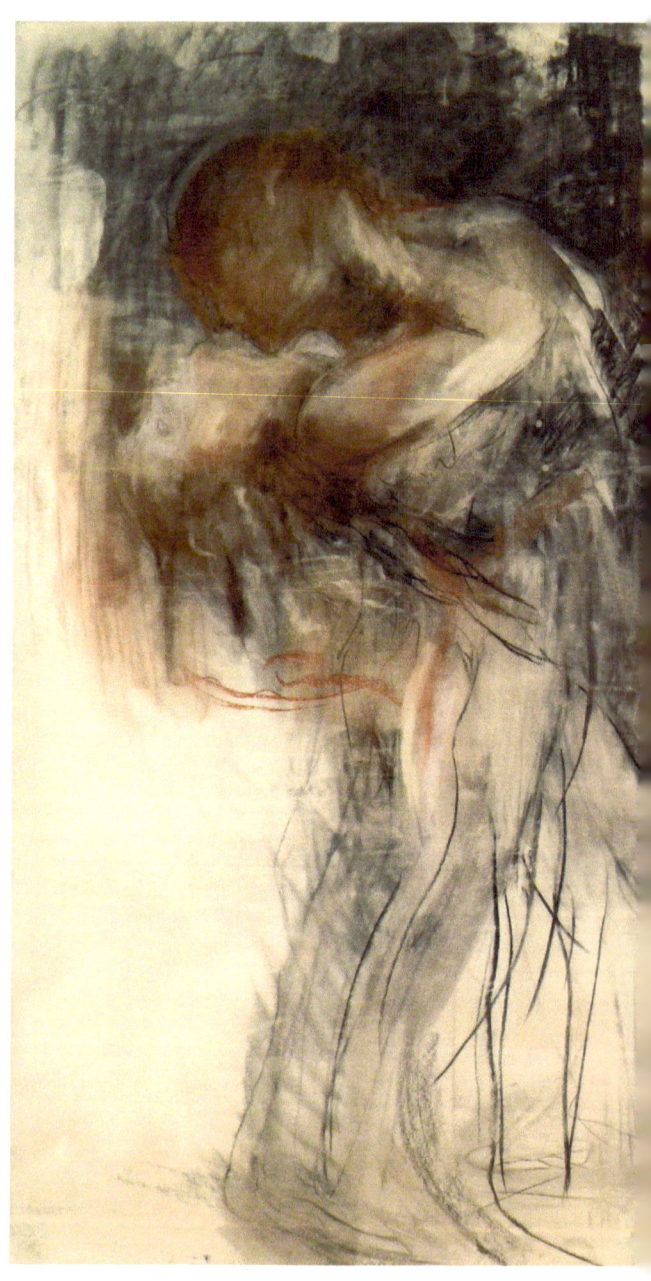

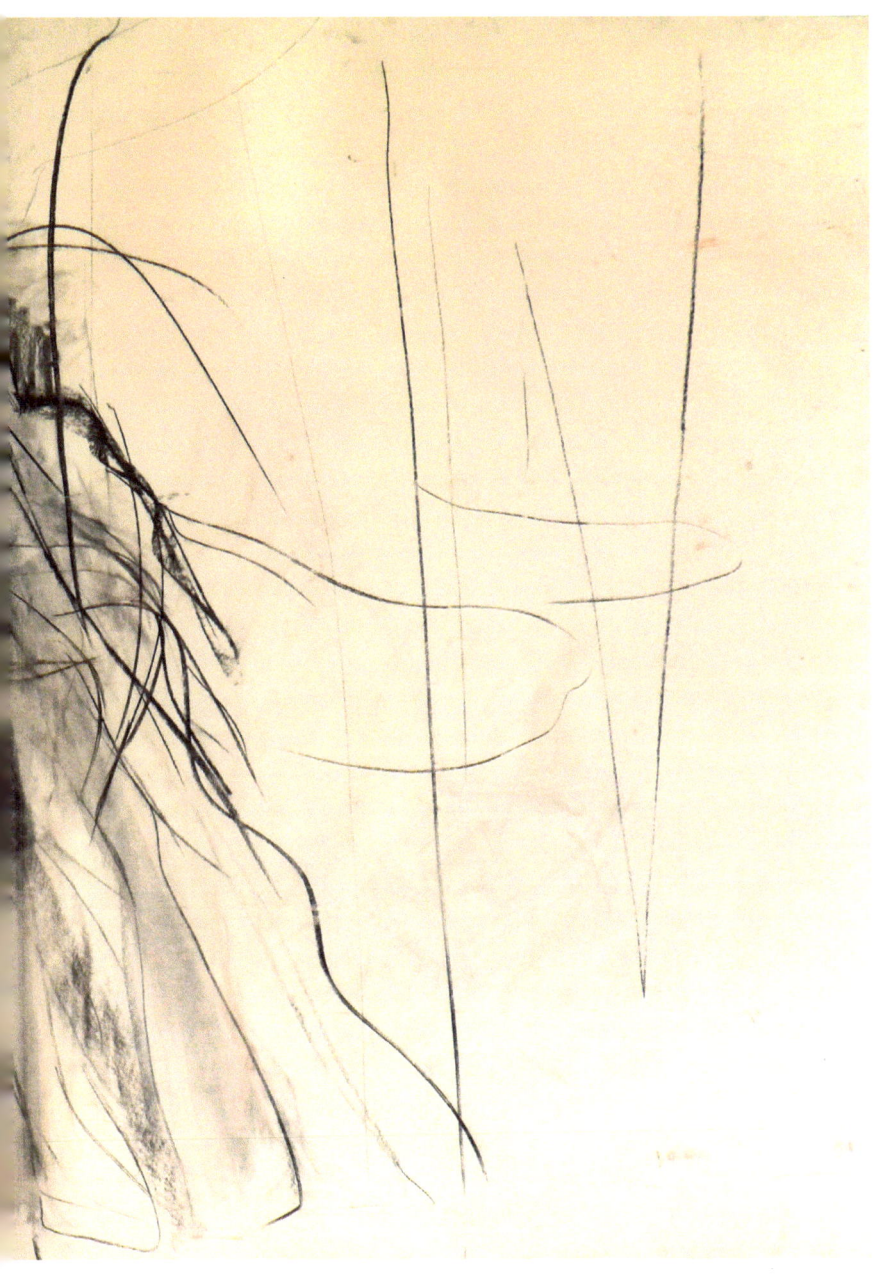

Jennifer Woodin
Binoculars, June 2011

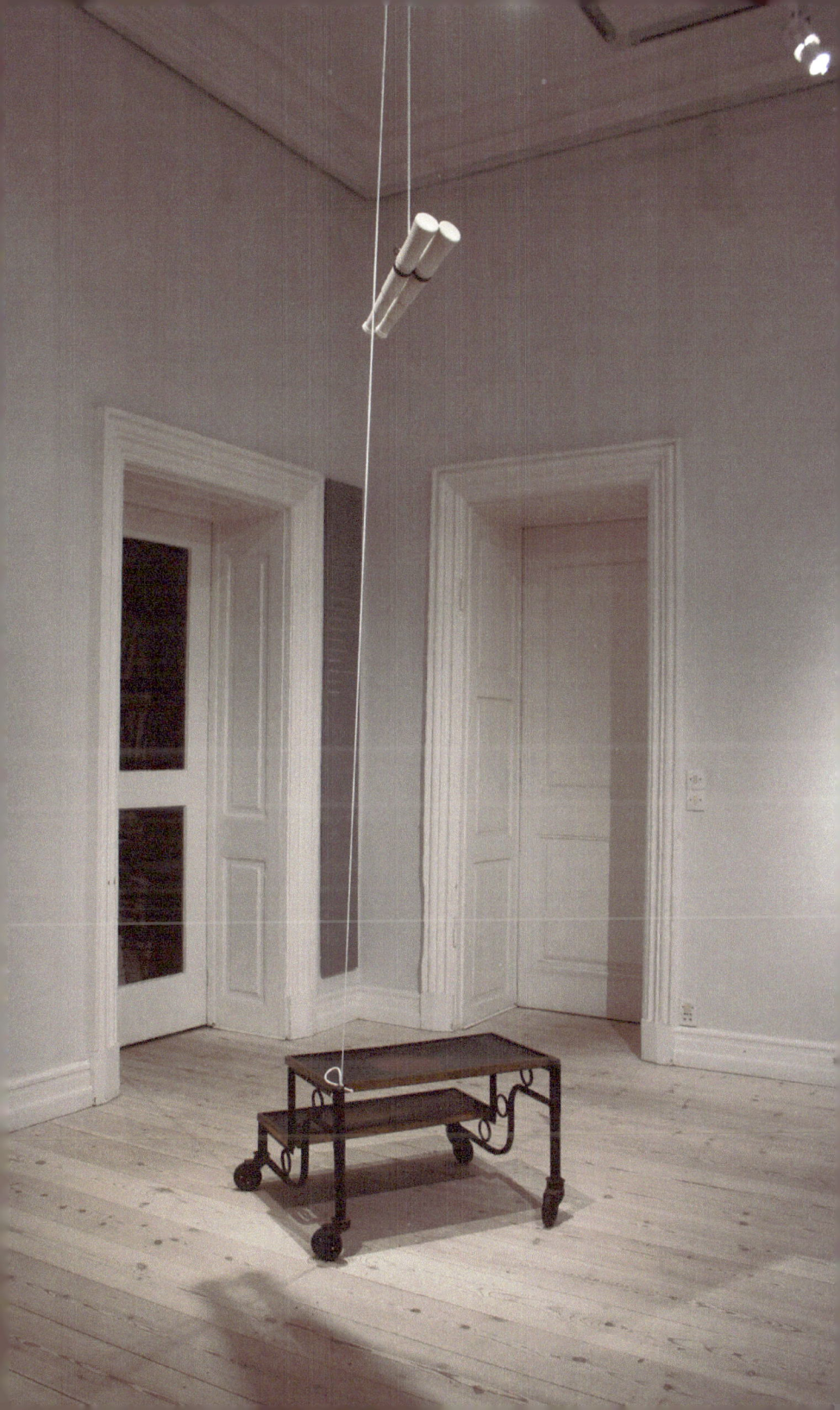

ABOUT
THE
ARTISTS

THOMAS ALBRECHT
Assistant Professor, Foundation

BFA Rhode Island School of Design
MAR Yale University
MFA University of Washington

www.thomasalbrecht.com

My performances explore ritual and language in public spaces, prodding cultural beliefs and individual doubts. Current projects involve duration and elements of absurdist theater, laying bare the provisional nature of human constructions and slippage between truth and fiction. Performance is an opportunity to work with time and contingency, with bodies acting in an ever-shifting world. We tinker and we cobble, we human creatures. Performance as a temporal activity is a personal check against artistic hubris. My work is nothing but a humble attempt to point at my stumbling about in the world, deconstructing and reconstructing and deconstructing and...

Thomas Albrecht has performed and exhibited throughout the United States and Europe and has initiated unscheduled interventions on sidewalks in multiple U.S. cities. His interactions with local police have been few.

ROBIN ARNOLD
Professor, Painting/Drawing

BFA Memphis State University
MFA Michigan State University

www.robinarnoldstudio.net

My works draw inspiration from botanical phenomena, both commonplace and anomalous. These are meditative pieces, searching out mysteries beyond the surface beauty of flora. My process is one of discovery— layering and taking away marks and images, excavating the mind, as well as apparent content. I favor indirect approaches; the strokes trace animating energy more than form. An edge of the synthetic or hyper-natural acknowledges our often mediated contemporary experience of nature.

JAMIE BENNETT
Professor, Metal

BBA   University of Georgia
MFA   State University of New York
at New Paltz

I have been interested for some time in how various cultures in changing eras have represented and mediated nature away from its natural state. I believe these interpretations are done to make nature resonate, whether through oppression, perfection, or interpretation. It is clear to me that the mediation of nature has a transcendent capability. In my most recent work there are careful, minutely detailed renderings of what could be living motifs but, paradoxically, are artificial and fragmented into unlikely abstracted topographies.

Jamie Bennett lives and works in Stone Ridge, New York, and is co-head of the Metal Program at the State University of New York at New Paltz. His work was the subject of a recent museum retrospective that traveled the United States from 2008–2010. His drawings, jewelry, and wall reliefs are in the collection of over twenty museums internationally, including the Victoria and Albert Museum; Hiko Misuno School of Jewelry Collection, Tokyo; the Musée des Arts Décoratifs,Paris; the Metropolitan Museum of Art, NYC; and the Yale University Art Gallery. He is a three-time recipient of a National Endowment for the Arts Fellowship. In 2009 the American Crafts Council named him Eileen Webb Fellow of the Council. In 2011 he was awarded his third New York Foundation for the Arts Fellowship. Professor Bennett has a one-person exhibition at Antonella Villanova Gallery, Florence, Italy, in May 2013.

STEVEN P. BRADFORD
Associate Professor, Sculpture

BA   Berea College
MFA   Rhode Island School of Design

Dead Man Shoes was made from shoes that I had found and saved in a building that I purchased and converted to a studio when living in Cleveland, OH. The shoes were items remaining in the building from the previous owner, who had died. I was interested in the idea of walking and dying and the Sisyphean likeness of life until death. The text from *Survival* originates from a 1968 Department of the Army Field Manual entitled *Survival Evasion and Escape*, which was left in a former church where I now reside. The text is overprinted reversed on top of the original text. The audio of the piece is a computer-generated reading of the text simultaneously forward and reversed. I am interested in negation that occurs from the same information and how that process is related to the original material.

RIMER CARDILLO
Professor, Printmaking

MFA   Instituto Escuela
      Nacional de Bellas Artes,
      Universidad de la
      República, Uruguay

www.rimercardillo.com

My concern for the survival of native peoples and preservation of natural ecosystems takes me to remote areas of the South American continent, such as El Pantanal, the Amazon region, or the rustic cattle ranches called *estancias* of the Uruguayan interior. Sketches and photographs collected over years of travel and fieldwork are the departure for my mixed-media works. These small sketches later are enlarged and carved into large pieces of wood, which are then printed over digital photographs from the Hudson Valley region. The silkscreen process and direct drawing allows me to create many different layers of colorful information that combine to form a unique work.

After receiving my degree, I spent two years in Germany studying at the Weissensee Kunst-Hochschule in Berlin and at the Hochschule für Grafik und Buchkunst in Leipzig. With a very strong background in printmaking, I have developed a large body of work that includes prints, sculptures, and installations. In 1997 I was awarded a John Simon Guggenheim Fellowship, and in 1998 The Bronx Museum of the

Arts exhibited a ten-year survey of my work. I was selected to represent Uruguay at the 2001 Venice Biennale with a large installation. In 2003 my cross-cultural interests were highlighted in a guest lecture at London's Tate Modern. In 2004 the Samuel Dorsky Museum of Art at SUNY New Paltz organized the first comprehensive survey of my career. In 2006 I received the Chancellor's Award for Excellence in Scholarship and Creative Activities, and the Research and Scholarship Award, Research Foundation, both from The State University of New York. The Museum Kiscell in Budapest, Hungary, exhibited a monumental installation at the Template Space in 2010. Recently the Nassau County Museum in Roslyn, Long Island, mounted *Jornadas de la Memoria*, a retrospective of my work, which was reviewed by Martha Schwendener in *The New York Times* ("Coded Messages," November 13, 2011).

I currently live and work in the Hudson Valley and in New York City.

AMY CHENG
Professor, Painting/Drawing

BFA   University of Texas at Austin
MFA   Hunter College, City
      University of New York

www.AmyChengStudio.com

My work is about visual play and visual pleasure. Sumptuous, intricate, ornamented, the paintings are richly referential. They call to mind a range of associations from mandalas, the cosmos, cells, lace, brocade, and more. I align myself with the long tradition of geometric and floral patterns the Far East, the Middle East, Byzantium, and the Baroque have long employed. They did so with the implicit understanding that pattern and repetition, which are endemic in nature, are primal in their rhythmic connection to the human nervous system.

BRYAN CZIBESZ
Assistant Professor, Ceramics

BA   Humboldt State University
MFA   San Diego State University

www.bryanczibesz.com

In this work, I have formalized the building blocks of technology as prototypical forms that explore the purpose—and result—of what we build in the physical environment. Known as the "Six Simple Machines," these building blocks (lever, inclined plane, wheel and axle, pulley, wedge, and screw represent the fundamental ways of demonstrating mechanical advantage (amount or direction of force) over the physiological limitations of our bodies.

Beginning with small explorations of form that retain a conspicuous record of their making, initial hand-built clay objects were digitally scanned and then reproduced as machined wax prototypes, transforming the evidence of my hand through an interpretation of both the eye and the hand of a machine. In preserving the record of this impermanent iteration, the wax prototypes were reproduced in vitreous porcelain and sugar. This reproduction parallels technological progression, which results in an incremental removal of the body and the introduction of increasingly refined materials, in the interest of overcoming limitations and alleviating physical arduousness.

Viewers are invited to explore the history of this process—from the marks of the hand through the interpretation of the hand of the machine—with their own senses. I have also revisited this process through the reconstruction of the forms as unfired earthenware icons, bringing the work back to the human body and highlighting the inherent contradictions present in technology, which is the manifestation of both our ability and desire to transcend the limitations of our physiology.

FRANÇOIS DESCHAMPS
Professor, Photography

BS   University of Illinois, Urbana
MS   Institute of Design, Chicago

www.francoisdeschamps.net

For much of my photographic career I have been interested in the use of imagination to create photographic narratives or poems. These works are inspired by summers spent in my studio located in an old funeral parlor on an island off the coast of Maine. I imagine the photographs made by a fictional Victorian photographer living in a similar old funeral parlor on a similar island off the coast of Maine. In all these images, the use of digital manipulation is paramount, but I hope subservient, to the idea explored.

Absence can create a potent sense of presence. Empty spaces, their subjects erased, await the departed actors' return. An abandoned hat rests uneasily on a paper mache ledge. Skin becomes paper. An apple becomes the starry emptiness of the night sky. The subjects fly out beyond the constraints of the frame. The emptiness is an antidote to our time of false plenty with its gaping hollow core

To create these images I use Victorian *cartes de visites*, predecessors of today's snapshots. I scan these small photographic cards used as gifts for family and friends one hundred years ago. In some, I eliminate the primary subject altogether to leave a pregnant space, eerily empty. In others, I have inserted my own photographs of objects that vacillate between absence and presence: an apple, skin, a plate, an empty display, and birds flying away.

JAMES FOSSETT
Assistant Professor, Foundation

BS   Kent State University

MFA School of the Museum of
Fine Arts, Boston
Tufts University

www.jamesfossett.com

I am a visual artist who works in video, photography, performance, sound, and installation. My work explores duration in both broad and specific applications of the term.

Three Women is from the *Jumpers* series, which is an extension of a project documenting swimming holes. The *Jumpers* series is about preserving those interchangeable moments of doubt, joy, and fear experienced in momentary flight. By stripping away the background those emotions are magnified, or at least isolated, by the absence of physical, geographical context.

Fossett's work is shown both nationally and internationally. A selection from his work on swimming holes was recently included in *International Photography Annual* 1, published by Manifest Press, 2012. He has participated in a number of artist residencies, including Ballinglen Arts Foundation in Ballycastle, Ireland. He has been awarded a Pro Arts Public Service Award from the City of Boston. Both the cities of Cambridge, MA, and Belmont, MA, commissioned Fossett to produce public murals.

Fossett is also a founding member of the performance group Cave Dogs. There he fills a multitude of roles, including those of producer, performer, videographer, editor, photographer, set designer, set builder, and light designer/technician.

As a member of Cave Dogs, Fossett has performed nationally and internationally. Additionally, with Cave Dogs Fossett has been awarded grants from The Henson Foundation, The NLT Foundation, and Franklin Furnace. The group is currently in production of the shadow performance *Sure-minded Uncertainties.*

ANDREA FRANK
Assistant Professor, Photography

DIPLOM Academy of Fine Arts,
        Munich, Germany
MFA   Parsons, The New School
        for Design
        Whitney Independent Study
        Program

www.andreafrank.net

I am interested in issues of global concern, the urgent need for change, and related aspects of collective psychology. My current focus is on the human impact on our environment and its broad range of effects. I am experimenting with harnessing methodologies and tools borrowed from System Dynamics and conduct my artistic research and production from this perspective. By exposing system boundaries and time horizons that are too narrowly defined and, as such, hinder our understanding of interrelated issues, I seek to challenge collective mental models and societal norms.

The work on display explores educational spaces at M.I.T., a prime driver in technological innovation. It is an examination of, and commentary on, conditions and traditions of modern learning. A juxtaposed group of calcified-looking plants— photographs of glass plant specimens from the Harvard Museum of Natural History, sandwich-mounted between two pieces of Plexiglas and laser-cut—hints at our distanced and fragmented understanding of natural systems currently under great stress due to human impact.

I joined SUNY New Paltz as Assistant Professor in the fall of 2012, and from 2003–2012 I taught Photography and Related Media as full-time lecturer in the MIT Program in Art, Culture and Technology in Cambridge, MA. Recent venues for solo exhibitions include Galleria Michela Rizzo, Venice, Italy; Carroll and Sons, Boston, MA; the Brevard Art Museum, Melbourne, FL; the MIT Museum, Compton Gallery, Cambridge, MA; and the Kunsthalle Göppingen, Göppingen, Germany.

MATTHEW FRIDAY
Assistant Professor,
Graduate Coordinator

BFA   University of New Mexico
MFA   Indiana State University
       Whitney Independent Study
       Program

www.matthewfriday.net

A Map Without Boundaries is a mobile research station containing a variety of cartographic and scientific instruments to measure the state of regional watersheds. This research station operates as a provisional laboratory, camping platform, library, and exhibition installation. *A Map Without Boundaries* can be applied to a variety of different watersheds with the goal of both registering the complex nature-culture relations that produce these environments and catalyzing new forms of agency within these entangled ecologies. *A Map Without Boundaries* also includes a mail art project published by Regional Relationships. The project asked participants to employ a set of specific conceptual tools to diagram their local watersheds.

I am an educator and transdisciplinary artist who works across a variety of media, contexts, and institutions. My research concerns the theory and implementation of radical pedagogy, regional ecologies, and the history and practice of communities of resistance. Working both collectively and individually, my projects have taken up issues of organized labor, community agriculture, and watershed remediation. I am an active member of the international research and consultation collective *spurse*.

Matthew Friday has exhibited in a number of venues including the Whitney Museum of American Art Open Studios; Center for Contemporary Arts, St. Louis, MO; Spaces, Cleveland, OH; MassMOCA, North Adams, MA; ArtSpace, Minneapolis, MN; Indianapolis Museum of Art; Grand Arts, Kansas City, MO; The Kitchen, NYC; Bemis Center for Contemporary Arts, Omaha, NB; and the BMW Guggenheim LAB, NYC. His work has been reviewed in *October*, the *New Art Examiner*, and *Dwell* and has been included in several catalogues, including *The Interventionists* (MassMOCA) and *Experimental Geography*.

KATHY GOODELL
Professor, Painting/Drawing

BFA   San Francisco Art Institute
MFA   San Francisco Art Institute

www.kathygoodell.com

I am interested in the expression "the naked eye," the eye unclothed, but of what? I have always been infatuated with lenses, optical devices, glass as a transmitter of light, accompanied by the organic world. I have used lenses sculpturally, photographically, and within painting installations.

The *Mesmer Oculus* series utilizes the painting installation *Mesmer Eyes*, a 24-foot long wall of 10,800 elliptical paintings with 21 freely suspended lenses as its subject matter. Shot through the suspended lenses, utilizing the dispersion and refraction of the images, and the aberrations, magnifications, and distortions of the painting wall, images are created that capture moments of the work.

With lenses we replicate a human organ, the eye, and the lenses see as we see, imperfectly, randomly, sometimes voraciously, and ever changing. We look through the lens of our eyes into another, larger, man-made lens, and our vision is shaped and deflected. We see everything in the vicinity— other viewers, the work reflected, the periphery—and we see it transformed in motion, as these lenses digest and distort. The *Mesmer Oculus* photos function as evidence of the multi-tiered process and complexity of the relationships in our lives.

RENA LEINBERGER
Lecturer, Foundation

BA   Anderson University
MFA School of the Art Institute
      of Chicago

www.renaleinberger.com

Rena Leinberger works primarily in sculpture, installation, public projects. and photography. The projects utilize building materials as object, image, and artifice, navigating our surroundings as simultaneously constructed and imaged space. She positions materials, images, and environments in duplicative and reciprocal relationships, producing an inquiry into material failure, progress, and the collapse of ideologies that accompany our architectures.

Rena Leinberger's work has been exhibited in solo shows at the Museum of Contemporary Art, Chicago; Gallery 400 at University of Illinois, Chicago; Zg Gallery, the Evanston Art Center, Evanston, Illinois; and 1R Gallery. Her work has been included in group shows internationally in Germany, Great Britain, and the United Arab Emirates. She has also been included in group exhibitions at Queens Museum of Art; Bronx Museum of the Arts; Smack Mellon, Brooklyn; Newhouse Center for Contemporary Art, Staten Island; CUE Art Foundation, NYC; MASS MoCA, North Adams; the Urban Institute of Contemporary Art, Grand Rapids, MI; and the City of San Antonio International Center,

among others. Her commissioned public project by the NYC DOT's Urban Art Program in Queens, New York, is currently on view. Awards include grants from the Joan Mitchell Foundation; a sponsored residency at the International Studio and Curatorial Program (ISCP) in New York; residencies at threewalls and Catwalk; and a fellowship in the Bronx Museum's Artist in the Marketplace program. She recently completed a residency in LMCC's Swing Space program on Governors Island, New York. Her work has been reviewed in *Sculpture Magazine*; *FiberArts*; *Chicago Tribune*; *Chicago Reader*; *New City*; *Artnet*; *ArtSlant*; *Bridge Magazine*; *mouthtomouth*; and *Brooklyn Rail*, among others.

CARMEN LIZARDO
Associate Professor, Foundation

BFA   Pratt Institute
MFA   Pratt Institute

My artwork has to do with multiple formal design elements, among which color is prominent. But there also are surface, shape, and feelings, which are more difficult to portray. I make diptychs using minimal color-field techniques, as well as representational portraiture, to represent the way in which the internal and external self relate to each other. In the abstract paintings color and form are merely instruments for creating conceptual portraits of mental states or feelings, such as fear, hate, love, anger, confusion, anxiety or joy, that arise as a subjective experience rather than as a conscious thought. In the work there is a basic reference to nature, and a highly articulated psychological use of color. While making the work, I remove myself from any direct contact, avoiding any kind of manipulation or mark making; I use droppers filled with different transparent pigments to carefully place a single drop in which there is no physical interference between gravity and the paper. One piece may be perfect while the next 10 fail, even when there is no environmental or physical change in the process. The paintings are small, measuring 5 by $3^1/_2$ inches, but when examined at close range, the scale of the object in the painting seems infinite in relation to the physical size of the whole piece.

The counterpart of the abstract work relies on the self-portraiture, done blindly, as I cannot predict what would it look like.

ANN LOVETT
Professor, Photography

BS   Skidmore College
MFA   Tyler School of Art,
      Temple University

www.annlovett.com

Employing the media of photography, artists' books, photo-encaustic processes, and writing, my creative practice reflects a poetic approach to the visual. Often drawing on history or the ephemera of museum collections, and more recently from the natural world, I am interested in constructing new meaning from what I see. This transformation may occur through the camera's lens, by layering images in wax, or in the way written language resonates in the pages of a bookwork. Visually rich and pleasurable, these works are also intended to question our perceptions of history and culture.

In recent photographs I have explored and documented aspects of the natural world, considering its power and vulnerability, as well as issues of preservation and use. Traveling in Iceland, Ireland, and Oregon, I developed this series of water studies, exploring light, space, and surface. Images from Iceland record the ephemeral qualities of light from long summer twilights and the residue of volcanic and glacial forces. In Ireland constantly changing weather reveals new patterns drawn by wind and rain. An Oregon winter sculpts lake surfaces as they settle, break apart, and reshape themselves. In these images water is both expansive and insistent, quietly claiming its space in our lives and our world. The photographs express my delight in its beauty, as well as my fears about the terrible vulnerability of this resource in a changing climate.

ALEÁNNA LUETHI-GARRECHT
Assistant Professor,
Graphic Design

BFA   Philadelphia College of Art
MFA EQUIVALENT
      Basel School of Design,
      Switzerland

The suspended fabric panels on display give an opportunity for fine art expression very different from my daily life as a graphic designer. They are tutorials. Two fabric panels from a series of five utilize typography as a textural medium. In the realm of design, texture is physical and it is imagined. Many of the textures that designers make use of are not physically experienced by the viewer at all, but exist as an optical effect and representation. I am interested in discovering letterform and typography as textural and rhythmic elements. I also am interested in historical and contemporary questions on the traditional use of typography, as well as new avenues of expression that allow typography, which normally is static, to become an unusually kinetic feature.

By trade and practice, I am both a graphic designer and a culinarian. My cultural and educational background spans the two continents of Europe and North America. The spine of who I am and what I create stems from my Swiss training in the International Typographic Style and Modernist theories and practice. Simplicity, making content intelligible and comprehensible, and instilling sensory exploration is the core of my work where typography is paramount.

MYRA MIMLITSCH-GRAY
Professor, Metal

BFA   Philadelphia College of Art
MFA   Cranbrook Academy of Art

www.mimlitschgray.com

I produce objects as portraits and social indicators. By implying or impeding function I reinterpret utility as a critical strategy. I create tableware that is both present and representational, embodying the specifics of the discipline, while also portraying its variant roles and circumstances. Deliberately tentative, this work investigates facture, explores gesture, and embodies utilitarian notions.

Myra Mimlitsch-Gray is a metalsmith who actively exhibits and lectures throughout the U.S. and abroad. She was awarded the 2012 United States Artists Fellowship in Craft and Traditional Arts. She also has been the recipient of Individual Artist Fellowships from the Louis Comfort Tiffany Foundation, the National Endowment for the Arts, and the New York Foundation for the Arts. In 1998 she received the Chancellor's Award for Excellence in Teaching at the State University of New York.

Mimlitsch-Gray's artwork is included in significant public collections, such as the Detroit Institute of Arts; the Metropolitan Museum of Art; the Museum of Arts and Design, the Smithsonian Institution; the Victoria and Albert Museum; and the Yale University Art Gallery. Her work has been published in *100 Treasures*, Cranbrook Art Museum, 2004; *Skilled Work: American Craft in the Renwick Gallery*, Smithsonian Institution Press, 1998; *Women Designers, 1900-2000: Diversity and Difference*, Yale University Press, 2000; and *One of a Kind: American Art Jewelry Today*, Abrams, 1995. The feature article "Of Hammers, History and Household: The Metalwork of Myra Mimlitsch-Gray," written by David McFadden, was published in *Metalsmith*, Spring 2005.

ITTY S. NEUHAUS
Associate Professor, Foundation

BFA   Pratt Institute
MFA   Tyler School of Art,
      Temple University

www.ittyneuhaus.com
www.vimeo.com/6958159

The mysteries held beneath the surface of the earth motivate much of my current work. Icebergs changed as I observed them while on a Fulbright in Newfoundland and Labrador over two sub-arctic summers. My aim is to reinvent the unseen underside of these monoliths, so as to reflect on their disappearance.

Neuhaus is grateful for recent opportunities with Esther Massry Gallery, Corporation of Yaddo, MacDowell Colony, CIES Fulbright Foundation, and Parks Canada.

AMY PAPAELIAS
Assistant Professor, Graphic Design / Foundation

BA   McGill University
MFA   State University of New York
      at New Paltz

www.amypapaelias.com
www.personatype.com

PersonaType: Living Type Specimens combines web fonts with user-generated web content (pillaged from posts, tweets and comments) to demonstrate the emotive qualities of type. These kinetic, or living, type specimens allow users to watch/listen to text speak/move in several sensory ways, making auditory and visible the personified characteristics that can be assumed by a typeface. The project serves as an experimental prototype to model methods for exploring the kinetic experience of web fonts and reimagining future reading experiences.

My work exists at the intersections of design, technology, and culture. My primary creative research in expressive typography and visual representations of speech challenge the arbitrary relationship between visual and verbal communication. A variety of tools are utilized, including font-editing software, handwriting samples, voice recordings, post-structuralist theory, sociolinguistics, and voice recognition technology. These projects have been recognized in a variety of online and print publications, including

>

AMY PAPAELIAS, continued

Print, Communication Arts, DesignObserver.com, Typographica. org, and have been used by developers at Microsoft, Adobe and Extensis to demonstrate the capabilities of OpenType font technology. I have presented my creative and pedagogical work at several national venues including TypeCon 2005, 2007, 2012; AIGA Design Educators Conference 2007; and UCDA Education Summit 2011. A faculty adviser for the AIGA Student Chapter at SUNY New Paltz and a member of the Type Directors Club of New York, I also am active professionally, collaborating with artists, small businesses, and non-profits on design for page and screen.

JILL PARISI
Assistant Professor, Printmaking

BFA   State University of New York
       at New Paltz
MFA   State University of New York
       at New Paltz

www.jillparisi.com

My work inspires a sense of wonder, a slowing down in the wake of increasingly fast-paced, screen-based lifestyles. The natural environment is an important part of my creative research. Study of botanical and zoological texts, along with observations in the field, inspire the fantastic flora and fauna inhabiting these works. The resulting "species" are introduced into various settings, and the components respond to most viewing spaces as the size and shape of the installations expand or contract in relation to their new habitat. Many of these works on paper are also interactive, as they respond to the flow of air within an exhibition space and are stirred into motion by the proximity of the viewer.

A selection of the artist's professional awards and achievements include a 2005 NYFA Fellowship in Printmaking, Drawing, and Artists Books; a Studio Immersion Project Fellowship at the Robert Blackburn Printmaking Workshop, 2010; a public art commission in hand-painted glass *Coom Barooom* for New York City's Metropolitan Transportation Authority's Arts for Transit program at Beach

44th Street in Rockaway, Queens, completed 2012; selection of her installation *Kaleidoscope Garden* for the Main Exhibition of the *Krakow 20th Printmaking Triennial* 2012, Krakow, Poland; and for the *Oldenburg Print Triennial* at the Horst-Janssen Museum, Oldenburg, Germany, 2013.

Current studio projects include engraved and hand-painted works on glass and a series of new sculptural prints and drawings. Parisi has been Assistant Professor of Printmaking at the State University of New York at New Paltz since 2007.

JESSICA POSER
Assistant Professor, Art Education

BA   University of Chicago
MFA   University of Illinois at Chicago

Noise refers to the process of video disambiguation or "snow." The primary materials used to make the pieces in this series are the cardboard packaging of cereal boxes and other household products, the residue of domestic consumption. The work articulates an exploration of the visual detritus or "noise" in domestic life, creating a landscape in which the viewer can meditate on the noise of contemporary visual and material culture.

Jessica Poser lives and works in the Hudson Valley.

EMILY PUTHOFF
Associate Professor, Sculpture

BFA   Ohio University
MFA   Arizona State University

www.emilyputhoff.com

The surround sound composition
is composed of Julia Alsaraff's
viola improvisations, crystal
singing bowls, and a factory
whistle. I met with Julia in an
historic, telescoping gas tank
in Troy, NY, and asked her to
visualize the form of a spiral,
ascending and descending, and
the relationship of harmony and
dissonance while she played. I
created the ceramic speakers
while an Artist-in-Residence at the
European Ceramic Work Centre in
s'Hertogenbosch, Netherlands.

Emily Puthoff's artwork
comprises sculpture, installation,
digital media, prints/drawings,
performance/interventions,
and artist books. Her work has
been recognized by numerous
grants, artist residencies, and
awards, including a 2011 New
York Foundation for the Arts
Artist's Fellowship in Digital and
Electronic Media and an Artist in
the Marketplace Fellowship at the
Bronx Museum for the Arts, as
well as artist residencies at the
European Ceramic Work Centre,
s'Hertogenbosch, Netherlands;
Women's Studio Workshop,
Rosendale, NY; Banff Art Centre,
Banff, Canada; and Sculpture
Space, Utica, NY. Her artwork has
been exhibited widely at museums
and galleries, including Neues
Kunstforum, Cologne, Germany;
The Bronx Museum of the Arts,
Bronx, NY; The Art House at the
Jones Center, Austin, TX; and The
Dorsky Museum, New Paltz, NY.

.

THOMAS SARRANTONIO
Assistant Professor, Foundation

BA   Fordham University
CERTIFICATE PAINTING
        Pennsylvania Academy of
        the Fine Arts
MA   University of Pennsylvania
MFA   State University of New York
        at New Paltz

www.thomassarrantonio.com

My paintings seek to mediate
between realms of external
perception and internal reflection.
They present themselves as
meditations on nature and
self. Choosing humble, often
overlooked, subject matter,
such as the overgrown grasses
at the edge of a field, I attempt
to translate the dynamic
processes of Nature into the
stasis of physical matter on a
painted surface. Small works are
produced directly from Nature,
while large paintings are studio
productions that utilize memory,
experience, imagination, and
conceptual ideas to negotiate the
terrain of contemporary painting.
The paintings are offered to the
viewer as templates to provoke
active participation in the process
of seeing and quiet contemplation
of the mysteries of consciousness.

Thomas Sarrantonio studied
painting at the Pennsylvania
Academy of the Fine Arts in
Philadelphia, where his teachers
included Will Barnet and Sidney
Goodman. His paintings have
been exhibited widely, and he is
the recipient of numerous honors,
including a Pollock-Krasner Award
and a Visiting Artist Residency
in Normandy, France. He lives in
Rosendale, New York, with his wife
and children.

ANAT SHIFTAN
Associate Professor, Ceramics

BA   Hebrew University, Jerusalem
MA   Eastern Michigan University
MFA   Cranbrook Academy of Art

My ceramic work investigates the relationship between human activity and natural growth and explores the representation of nature in art. While I consider the forms of my hand-painted porcelain vases to be modern, my drawing and glazing techniques are based on traditional methods. Prior to their firing, each of the columnar vases is glazed with cobalt blue, manganese brown, and black brushwork. I work directly from botanical illustrations of plants found in Wave Hill's Wild Garden to create the representations of plant species on each vase. Through this process, my botanical drawings on porcelain strike a balance between exactness and imprecision that mimics the simultaneous constraint and abandon of the Wild Garden.

An Israeli artist whose work often speaks through floral and zoological imagery, Shiftan has exhibited internationally, including at The Clay Studio, Philadelphia, PA; Greenwich House Pottery, Greenwich, CT; Jingdezhen Ceramic Institute, Jingdezhen, China; and the Eretz Israel Museum, Tel Aviv, Israel. She also has participated in the 12th International Raku Workshop at OLR-Plemenitas, Zagreb, Croatia.

SUZANNE STOKES
Associate Professor, Foundation

BFA   Kent State University
MFA   State University of New York
      at New Paltz

www.cavedogs.org

Several years ago I began to develop a new body of work based on my prior investigations of shadow and video projection in the theater through my work with Cave Dogs, which takes its shape as multimedia, collaborative, shadow-based performance. New shadow projection drawings and intricate paper cut-outs emerged as a response to the healing process I experienced after a traumatic accident. Through drawing, I systematically documented each face and the hands of the numerous people who directly aided in the healing process of my then injured hand and wrist. The imagery from these two aspects of my work directed me to explore a variety of printmaking techniques, which led to a series of monotypes. Traditional and digital printmaking techniques are combined with the press to print monotypes made from a series of layered vellum stencils and natural materials.

The current work of Suzanne Stokes examines the nature of existence on the physical and metaphysical planes through the divergent lenses of micro and macro perspectives. The integration and interaction of the figure with nature looks at how the interplay of relationships, spiritualism, and stewardship of the earth shape our modern world. The contemplation that occurs between many of the figures shows a reflection and conscious awareness of family, generational cycles, loss, mortality, and ultimately a buoyant, soaring freedom. These visual investigations focus on how light and shadow defines, reveals, and conceals the form of the human body and its surrounding environments. The work forms a collective narrative that addresses mankind's complicated relationship to nature and each other.

Suzanne Stokes lives and works in Bloomington, New York. Her performance, installation, and print work has been shown nationally and internationally. She is the founder and artistic director of the theatrical performance group Cave Dogs. She also fills a multitude of roles, including those of lighting designer and technician, performer, choreographer, writer, and prop, costume, and set designer and maker.

With Cave Dogs, Suzanne has performed nationally and internationally at venues including The Malmo Cultural Festival, Sweden; Friskolen 70, Copenhagan, Denmark; P.S. 122, NYC; Henry Street Settlement; NYC; HERE, NYC; Mobius, Boston, MA; and The Center for Contemporary Art, Santa Fe, NM. In addition, Cave Dogs has received multiple grants from The Jim Henson Foundation, NYC; Franklin Furnace, NYC; and The NLT Foundation, Boston, MA. The group is currently in production of the shadow performance *Sureminded Uncertainties.*

ALICE WEXLER
Professor, Art Education

BFA   Boston University
MFA   Royal College of Art, London
EDD   Columbia University,
        Teachers College

I am an artist and art educator working in the fields of disability and outsider art. The social and political implications of disability and the crossing of boundaries among fields are often the subjects of my research. In 2007 as a visiting scholar at the Australian Institute for Aboriginal and Torres Strait Islander Studies (AIATSIS), I researched the art of children from the Stolen Generation in Southwestern Australia. Data from this research was published as an article in *Studies in Art Education*, "Koorah Coolingah—Children Long Ago: Art from the Stolen Generation." A monograph *Art and Disability: The Social and Political Struggles Facing Education* was published by Palgrave Macmillan in 2009, and a compendium *Art Education Beyond the Classroom: Pondering the Outsider and Other Sites of Learning* was published in 2012, also by Palgrave Macmillan.

In addition, I have written several articles on the subject of disability for art education journals. Most recently I published "The Siege of the Cultural City Is Underway: Adolescents with Developmental Disabilities Make 'Art,'" in *Studies in Art Education*. In summer 2012 I was invited to attend the inaugural forum *Examining the Intersection of Arts Education and Special Education* at the Kennedy Center and to participate in the planning for next summer's session. A professional paper I wrote "Art, Developmental Disabilities, and Self-Representation" was recently published by the Kennedy Center in 2013 for a collection of professional papers *The Intersection of Arts Education and Special Education: Exemplary Programs and Approaches*.

CHERYL WHEAT
Lecturer, Foundation

BFA State University of New York at Purchase
MFA Brooklyn College

www.cherylwheat.com

My recent large-scale drawings present a mythic view of the universe. I am fascinated by the handcraft of drawing and the raw materials. Having lived in Rome, I sense the timelessness of beauty in an ephemeral world. My drawings are not about the representation of forms, but rather the way in which I experience forms. Drawing may convey more to the imagination than an accurate reflection of an external reality. The nature of drawing, for me, is an expression of the unseen: touch, time, sound, pressure, and gravity. In the smallest element of a drawing one can have a partial intuition of the whole world. I desire to get at the psycho-physical qualities of forms. In poetry, as in drawing, there must be such things as unverifiable truths. I wish to create a visual language, like that of poetry, where the distance from the real world is great and sensibilities are heightened.

JENNIFER WOODIN
Assistant Professor, Ceramics and Foundation

BS California State University, Chico
MFA University of Oregon

www.jenniferwoodin.com

Originally from California, Jennifer Woodin is an artist/designer and educator working in the field of ceramics and emergent technologies. She received a BS in mechanical engineering and went on to have an eight-year career in both mechanical and civil engineering. Interested in a career in the arts, Woodin received her MFA in 2007. Her research and practice combine aspects of her two careers that form a unique line of inquiry.

In 2011 Woodin received an Artist-in-Residence Award at Statens Værksteder for Kunst (Danish National Arts Studio) in Copenhagen, Denmark. She has presented lectures at Tyler School of Art; Kansas City Art Institute; Alberta College of Art and Design; NCECA; and the H.O.P.E.S. conference for the Ecological Design Center, Eugene, Oregon. Woodin has exhibited nationally and globally, including 221A Gallery, Vancouver, BC; Meneer de Wit Gallery, Amsterdam; *Taiwan Biennial*, Taipei; Grimmerhus Museum, Middlefort, Denmark; Jordan Schnitzer Museum of Art, Eugene, Oregon; Svinvik Arboretum, Surnadal, Norway; and various other locations.

CHECKLIST

CHECKLIST
All works courtesy of the artist unless otherwise noted.

THOMAS ALBRECHT
Tinker, 2013
Wood table and chair, books, paper, drawing materials
Variable dimensions

ROBIN ARNOLD
Midnight Sun, 2011
Oil on canvas
60 x 66 inches

Countdown, 2010
Charcoal, graphite, pastel on paper
50 x 38 inches

Wall Garden, 2013
Graphite, charcoal, ink, colored pencil, and pastel on paper
Variable dimensions

JAMIE BENNETT
Queste #21, Brooch, 2012
Enamel, gold, copper
2$^{1}/_{2}$ x 3 inches

6th Matter of Appearance, Brooch, 2011
Enamel, silver, copper
3$^{1}/_{4}$ x 3$^{1}/_{4}$ inches
Courtesy of Sienna Gallery, Lenox, MA

12th Matter of Appearance, Brooch, 2011
Enamel, gold, copper
3$^{1}/_{4}$ x 3$^{1}/_{4}$ inches
Courtesy of Sienna Gallery, Lenox, MA

Untitled, 2011
Watercolor, ink, pencil on paper
13$^{7}/_{8}$ x 16$^{3}/_{8}$ inches
framed

Untitled, 2011
Watercolor, ink, gouache on paper
13$^{7}/_{8}$ x 16$^{3}/_{8}$ inches
framed

Untitled, 2011
Watercolor, ink, pencil on paper
18$^{3}/_{4}$ x 16$^{1}/_{8}$ inches
framed
Courtesy of Arthur Hash and Liz Clark

STEVEN P. BRADFORD
Dead Man Shoes, 2007
Mechanical, found, and constructed elements
98 x 46 inches

Survival, 2012
Inkjet print on vintage paper, computer generated audio
17$^{1}/_{2}$ x 14$^{1}/_{2}$ x 1$^{1}/_{2}$ inches
(excluding headphones)

RIMER CARDILLO
Gus and Pond Reflections II, from the series *From the Estancias to the Hudson Valley*, 2009
Digital photograph, woodcut, drawing, silk-screen, unique proof on paper
47$^{1}/_{2}$ x 35$^{1}/_{2}$ inches

Other Gus with Shawangunk Mountains, from the series *From the Estancias to the Hudson Valley*, 2011
Digital photograph, woodcut, drawing, silk-screen, unique proof on paper
47$^{1}/_{2}$ x 35$^{1}/_{2}$ inches

Criollo Horses in Grass-land, from the series *From the Estancias to the Hudson Valley*, 2010
Digital photograph, woodcut, drawing, silk-screen, unique proof on paper
48 x 35$^{3}/_{4}$ inches

AMY CHENG
Topkapi, 2011
Oil on canvas
28 x 36 inches

Broaching the Subject, 2012
Oil on canvas
38 x 41 inches

BRYAN CZIBESZ
Prototype: Wheel (Platonic, Production, Consumable, and Iconic Forms), 2011–13
Digital print, machinable wax, porcelain, sugar, terracotta
Variable dimensions

FRANÇOIS DESCHAMPS
The Absence of Presence, 2013
Pigment prints, framed
Variable dimensions

JAMES FOSSETT
Three Women, 2011
Archival inkjet on paper
18 x 12 inches

Group (jump), 2011
Archival inkjet on paper
18 x 12 inches

Boy (flop), 2011
Archival inkjet on paper
18 x 12 inches

Woman Diver, 2011
Archival inkjet on paper
18 x 12 inches

Girl (with hair), 2012
Archival inkjet on paper
18 x 12 inches

Man (screaming), 2012
Archival inkjet on paper
18 x 12 inches

ANDREA FRANK
Plant #1, 2012
Laser-cut, sandwich-mounted archival pigment print from photographs taken from the Blaschka Glass Flowers on display at the Harvard Museum of Natural History
9 x 7 inches

Untitled # 1, 2, 3, 4, 5, 6, 7, 8, and 9, from the series *Flora*, 2012
Laser-cut, sandwich-mounted, archival pigment prints
Circa 7 x 8 x 3/8 inches each

Untitled # 1, 3, 4, and 8, from the series *Classrooms*, 2011
Archival pigment print
12 x 15 1/16 inches each

MATTHEW FRIDAY
A Map Without Boundaries, 2009–ongoing
Provisional research laboratory, prototype stirling engine, Fresnel lens, watershed testing equipment, diagrams made from remediated water pollutants, PVC panel mounted on wood
Variable dimensions

KATHY GOODELL
Oculus Maw, 2012
Handmade glass lens, steel, monofilament
Variable height x 15 x 15 inches

Mesmer Oculus #7, 2012
Archival pigment print, acrylic glass, aluminum
42 x 60 x 2 inches

Mesmer Oculus #11, 2012
Archival pigment print, acrylic glass, aluminum
42 x 60 x 2 inches

Pneuma # 6, 2012
Ink, enamel on synthetic paper
26 x 40 inches

RENA LEINBERGER
Utopias, Unmoored, 2012
Rubber, foam, paint, paper, projector, digital video
Variable dimensions

CARMEN LIZARDO
Equivalent #1 to #12, 2013
Ink on paper, photographs
5 x 3 1/2 inches each

ANN LOVETT
Untitled (Kerlingarfjöll, Iceland), 2011
Archival pigment print
22 x 22 inches

Untitled (Newbliss, Ireland), 2011
Archival pigment print
22 x 22 inches

Untitled (Sisters, Oregon), 2012
Archival pigment print
22 x 22 inches

Untitled (Sisters, Oregon), 2012
Archival pigment print
22 x 22 inches

Untitled (Sisters, Oregon), 2012
Archival pigment print
22 x 22 inches

Untitled (Skagaströnd, Iceland), 2012
Archival pigment print
22 x 22 inches

ALEÁNNA LUETHI-GARRECHT
Lineform and Letterform: Typography in Textural Experiences, June 2012
Silkscreen on fabric
8 feet x 44 inches

MYRA MIMLITSCH-GRAY
Clove Oval, 2010
Copper, brass
4 x 14 x 8 inches

Wooden, 2007
Fabricated brass
14 x 40 x 17 inches

Four-Handled Skillet, 2007
Cast ductile iron
2 x 25 x 15 inches

Ink Study for Wooden, 2006
Ink on paper
22 x 30 inches

ITTY S. NEUHAUS
Whelmed in Deeper Gulfs with Words, 2010–2012
Ink, dye and Caran d'Ache water soluble crayons on heavy weight tracing paper and collaged rice paper mounted on light box/frame
34 x 34 inches
35 x 35 x 4 5/16 inches framed

Scratch Berg, 2011
Vellum archival inkjet print, lines removed by scratching
25 7/16 x 34 3/8 inches
35 x 44 inches framed

AMY PAPAELIAS
PersonaType: Living Type Specimens, 2012
Website
(www.personatype.com)

JILL PARISI
Kaleidoscopic Infloresence, 2013
Drawing, intaglio, lithographic prints on loktah, kizukishi, gampi, mitsumata tissues
Variable dimensions x 2 inches relief from wall

JESSICA POSER
Birth of the Universe, Parts I-VI, from the series *Noise*, March 2012
Recycled cardboard on wood panel
20 x 20 inches, each panel

EMILY PUTHOFF
We are floating in a medium of vast extent (excerpt from Pascal's *Pensées*), 2007–2013
Custom-made ceramic speakers, 10-minute surround-sound composition

THOMAS SARRANTONIO
Swarm, 2012
Oil on canvas
30 x 30 inches

Path, 2012
Oil on canvas
30 x 30 inches

Paysage, 2013
Oil on canvas
30 x 30 inches

Milieu, 2010
Oil on wood panel
12 x 12 inches

ANAT SHIFTAN
Celadon and Bronze, 2006
Porcelain
12 x 17 x 3 inches each

Untitled, from the series *Garden Views*, 2006
Porcelain
16 x 10 inches each

Untitled, from the series *Garden Views*, 2006
Porcelain
18 x 12 inches each

Still Life with Vase and Branch, 2010
Porcelain
16 x 10 x 8 inches

Still Life with Two Apples, 2010
Porcelain
6 x 10 x 8 inches

SUZANNE STOKES
Kindred Spirits, 2012
Thirteen prints: oil-based printing ink, Rives BFK, Japanese paper
$8\frac{1}{2}$ x 6 feet

ALICE WEXLER
Charlie 1, June 2012
Inkjet print on paper
42 x 30 inches

Charlie 2, June 2012
Inkjet print on paper
42 x 30 inches

My Summer Vacation, June 2012
Video

Charlie Appropriating Duchamp Appropriating a Bottle Rack, November 2012
Metal bottle rack, plastic bottles
$22\frac{1}{2}$ inches high x $15\frac{1}{2}$ inches diameter

CHERYL WHEAT
Hypnerotomachia, 2012
Chalk, pastel, paint on paper
60 x 80 inches

JENNIFER WOODIN
Binoculars, June 2011
Porcelain and leather
Variable dimensions

His and Hers, 2011
Insulation foam, plexiglas
40 x 18 x 6 inches

www.ingramcontent.com/pod-product-compliance
Lightning Source LLC
Chambersburg PA
CBHW040904180526
45159CB00010BA/2927